ALBERT EI

MARIE C......

MORSE CODE

GUGLIELMO MARCONI

FRANCIS CRICK, JAMES WATSON AND MAURICE WILKINS

INSECT REPELLENT

ALEXANDER FLEMING

MOLECULAR MACHINES

TU YOUYOU

SUBRAHMANYAN CHANDRASEKHAR

RADIATION

GERTRUDE ELION

PENICILLIN

NORMAN BORLAUG

RITA LEVI-MONTALCINI

JEAN-PIERRE SAUVAGE, FRASER STODDART AND BERNARD FERINGA

CELLS   BARRY MARSHALL AND ROBIN WARREN

HOW TO WIN A
NOBEL PRIZE

FROM NOBEL PRIZE-WINNER

BARRY MARSHALL

WITH LORNA HENDRY

ILLUSTRATIONS BY BERNARD CALEO

ROCK THE BOAT

A Rock the Boat Book

First published by Rock the Boat,
an imprint of Oneworld Publications, 2019

ISBN 978-1-78607-524-6
eISBN 978-1-78607-525-3

Text design and typesetting by Marilyn de Castro
Author photographs by Sharon Smith (pp. 53, 82, 178, 179);
Tania Jovanovic (p. 180) and Tiffany Garviev (p. 181)
Printed and bound in Great Britain by Clays Ltd, Elcograf S.p.A.

Oneworld Publications
10 Bloomsbury Street
London WC1B 3SR

Stay up to date with the latest books,
special offers, and exclusive content from
Rock the Boat with our monthly newsletter

Sign up on our website
www.rocktheboat.london

MIX
Paper from
responsible sources
FSC® C018072

CONTENTS

1

THE SECRET SOCIETY

Mary was bored. Her mother had let her come to this meeting to meet a famous scientist, but he wasn't even here yet. Everyone was just sitting around a big table, drinking coffee and eating biscuits and fiddling with their phones.

"I'm so sorry," said a blonde woman called Josephine, who seemed to be in charge. "Professor Marshall does sometimes lose track of time."

Mary nudged her mother. "Is that the man who won the Nobel Prize?"

Mary's mother nodded and frowned at the same time, which Mary knew meant that she was supposed to be quiet.

Ever since Mary was very young, she had wanted to win a Nobel Prize. She loved doing science experiments at home. Once she had built a boat for her bath that was powered by a balloon. Another time she had made a cloud appear in a glass jar. When Mary overheard her mother say that she would be visiting an important research centre and meeting a scientist who had won a Nobel Prize, she had nagged for days to be allowed to come. But now nothing was happening and the scientist wasn't even here.

"Can I go for a walk?" she whispered.

Her mother nodded again.

Mary slipped out of the nearest door, grabbing a biscuit on the way. She wandered along a long corridor, stopping sometimes to stand on her tiptoes and peer through windows into brightly lit laboratories where people wearing long white coats were doing things with test tubes and impressive machines with lots of dials and lights and numbers.

At the very end of a winding corridor, just as she was getting bored again, she noticed a door with a handwritten sign stuck to it. It read:

Mary knew that one thing all scientists had in common was curiosity. So, very carefully, she turned the door handle and pushed the door open, just a crack.

"Albert! You know the rules! We may only discuss science. Not our personal lives or world affairs, no matter how interesting they are." It was a woman's voice, and she sounded annoyed.

"But rules are made to be broken! That's why most of us are here. If we'd obeyed the rules, we never would have made the breakthroughs we did."

Mary ducked down and peeked around the door, being careful to stay out of sight. More than anything else, she loved listening to grown-ups arguing. She found out a lot of very interesting things that way.

Unlike the laboratories, this room was dark and windowless. It looked more like a storage room than a place where important meetings were held. The only light came from a bare lightbulb that hung from the centre of the ceiling. About twenty people, many of them dressed quite strangely, were sitting on wooden boxes or milk crates or upturned buckets. An old whiteboard was propped up against the back wall and, luckily for Mary, everyone was looking at it. A man in a crumpled lab coat was busy drawing on the board with a green marker.

Mary crept in through the doorway and hid behind a box of cleaning cloths.

"So, here's our idea. Robin and I think that we might be able to use the bacteria that we discovered to vaccinate everyone in the world against malaria."

"Still no cure for cancer, though," said a tired looking man in a hospital gown.

"No, Ralph. Sorry."

A woman with a very stern face snorted. "That'd be right."

"Rosalind, don't complain. By rights you

shouldn't even be here anyway," said a man with wild white hair that stuck out from his head as if he'd had an electric shock. "Not that I care about the rules, mind you!"

Mary stared at him. He looked very familiar. She had a poster on her bedroom wall of someone who looked just like that. The same smiling eyes above the same bushy moustache. But her poster was of Albert Einstein and he had been dead for years. It couldn't be him. Could it?

Mary crawled around the side of the box she was hiding behind, trying to get closer so she could see better in the dim light. Her foot knocked a broom that was leaning against the wall and it came crashing down on top of her.

"Oww!" she cried, rubbing her head where the broom had whacked her. "That hurt!"

She stood up crossly, to see all twenty people staring at her in shock.

"Is one of you Professor Marshall?" asked Mary. "Because I came here to meet you but you're late. Everyone's waiting for you in the boardroom."

The man standing at the whiteboard checked his watch. "Yes, that's me. I always forget about the

time when we get talking. We'll have to wrap this up. I think our next meeting is at Fleming's place." He pulled out a small gold orb from his pocket and peered at it. "Now, Mary, just remind me. How do I send everyone back to their own time?"

"I'm Mary," said Mary. "But I don't know what you're talking about."

Professor Marshall looked up at her. "No, you can't be. At least not yet—"

A woman holding a scarf across her face whispered urgently into the man's ear.

"I suppose you're right," said Barry. "This is awkward. But she's seen us now. We can't undo that."

"We'll have to swear her to secrecy," said an elderly woman with glasses.

"Or pay her off," said a tall, well-dressed man with a long face and short slicked-back hair.

"Who are you people?" asked Mary. There was an awkward silence. "Because *you* look just like Albert Einstein." She pointed at the man with the crazy white hair. He grinned at her.

"Correct!"

"But ... you're ..." Mary hesitated.

"Dead?" he offered. "Yes, in your time. It's the

wonder of time travel. In fact in your time most of us here are dead. Not our host, Barry, of course." He gestured at Professor Marshall, who nodded his head in agreement. "Or Tu here." Einstein pointed to the woman with glasses. "She's quite new. She only joined our secret society of Nobel Prize winners a couple of years ago. And these three gentlemen are at their first meeting. We were just explaining the rules to them. No discussions about anything but science and no telling people things about their own future. Rules, rules, rules. It's so boring."

"Albert! Stop talking!" A woman in an old black dress looked despairingly at Einstein.

Mary wasn't sure what to think – *time travel?* But she knew that scientists had to keep an open mind ...

"So why did you want to meet me?" Professor Marshall asked Mary.

"Because I want you to tell me how I can win a Nobel Prize," said Mary. She looked around the room. "All of you! I want to know how you did it. And ..." She hesitated, not sure if the idea that had just popped into her head was very good or very, very bad. "And if you don't, I'll tell everyone about your secret society!"

Professor Marshall sighed. He looked at the woman with the scarf, who had almost completely disappeared into the shadows at the back of the room. She nodded.

"Very well. But do you mind waiting outside for a minute?"

Mary agreed, relieved and also a bit surprised that her plan had worked, and she went back out to the corridor. From behind the closed door she heard loud talking and a bit of arguing, but then there was a flash of bright light, everything went quiet and Professor Marshall opened the door. The room behind him was completely empty.

"We drew straws," he said. "You can visit eleven people in their own time and ask them your question. But then you have to keep our secret forever. How does that sound?"

"Great! Thank you, Professor."

"Call me Barry," he said. "Now, are you ready to get started?"

"Now? But you're already late for your meeting."

"Yes, but I have a time machine!" He frowned at the gold orb in his hand. "I think this is right," he muttered. "Let's see."

He pressed a button on the orb. The whole
world whirled around the two of them and they
were surrounded by light. For a brief moment Mary
saw a blur of corridor, door and – inexplicably –
stars, and then everything disappeared.

NOBEL PRIZE

Alfred Nobel was a Swedish scientist, inventor and businessman. His most famous invention was an explosive called dynamite. He also invented gelignite, a detonator and the blasting cap. In 1864 his factory exploded, killing his brother and several other people. The work he did was very dangerous, but he hoped that the powerful explosives and ammunition he was making would help to bring an end to war.

When Nobel died in 1896 he left behind a large fortune. In his will, he surprised his family by stating that the money be used to establish prizes to reward people who had done their best to benefit humanity. The five categories he named were Physics, Chemistry, Physiology or Medicine, Literature and Peace.

The first Nobel prizes were awarded in 1901. The name 'Nobel', which once made people think of explosives and destruction, is now associated with science, art and peace.

2

EVERYTHING IS RELATIVE

Albert Einstein

Mary and Barry were standing in the middle of a child's bedroom. A little boy was sitting cross-legged on the floor, staring intently at a compass.

"Ah, we're too early," said Barry, looking down at the time machine. "My mistake." He spun the dial and pressed the button again, the bedroom whirled violently around them, and suddenly they were in a small medical laboratory.

Barry peered at the time machine. "Oops. 1973. Too late. Let me try to get this right."

Mary looked around the laboratory as Barry studied the dial. On a wooden bench sat a large glass jar. It was full of a dirty yellow liquid, and suspended in the liquid was something that looked suspiciously like— "Is that someone's *brain*?" she asked.

Barry glanced up. "Ah, not just 'someone's'. It's Albert Einstein's. The doctor who did the autopsy after Einstein died stole it. He wanted to study it to see what made Einstein so brilliant. It turns out that Einstein's brain is pretty much the same as everyone else's. It's what he did with his brain that was extraordinary."

As Mary digested all that, Barry hooted in triumph. "Got it! I think I'm finally getting the hang of this thing." He pushed the button again and they were transported to a tiny office that held a small desk piled high with papers.

Barry whispered, "This may not be the best time either. I think we've interrupted him at work. We're in Switzerland in 1905."

A man with curly dark hair and a thick moustache suddenly popped up from behind the papers and smiled brightly at them. "Mary!" he said. "So nice of you to drop in again. But you've shrunk!"

Barry frowned at him. "Albert. She's still only ten."

"Of course! My mistake. I'm confused. I've got a lot on my mind. All this work ..." He gestured vaguely at the pile of papers around him.

"You must have a very important job, Mr Einstein," said Mary politely, trying very hard to forget that she had just seen his brain floating in a jar.

"Oh, my job is easy. I get it all done before my morning coffee. No, I'm working on some very important scientific papers this year. This one here," and Einstein waved a notepad covered in scribbles, "is my masterpiece. The first one, anyway. There will be a few more. This is my special theory of relativity. Here, look at this, Mary." He swept a pile of papers to the floor and plonked a mug on the desk. "Where is my coffee cup? On the left or the right of my desk?"

"On the right," said Mary.

"But not for me!" Einstein cried from the other side of the desk. "Come round here. For me, it's on the left. Do you see? Everything is relative to where *you* are."

Mary glanced at Barry. "Sure, but that seems kind of . . . obvious."

"Yes, yes, yes. But let's add in motion. What if that coffee cup is on a spaceship and it's moving past you. If you're standing still, you can measure how fast it's travelling, right? Easy! But what if you're on another spaceship and you're going in a different direction? What then? All you can do then is work out how the cup is moving relative to you and your motion. Until now, everyone assumed there was some kind of fixed position and you could measure all motion from that spot. But it's not true. *Everything* is relative! Space! Motion! Even time! Except the speed of light. Interestingly, that never changes. Light travels at 299,792,458 metres per second no matter where you are in the universe or how fast you're moving. And nothing can travel faster than light. It's the ultimate speed limit."

"Yes, the speed of light is annoying, actually," said Barry. "It's going to make space travel very difficult. It takes way too long to get anywhere interesting."

"Yes, unfortunately it's a constant," said Einstein. "That's why I call it 'c' in my most famous equation: $E = mc^2$. I've proved that energy and mass are just different forms of the same thing. Energy can become mass! Mass can become energy!"

"That's basically what happens in an atomic bomb," said Barry helpfully.

Einstein's moustache drooped and he suddenly looked sad. "Don't remind me."

"But at least you won the Nobel Prize," said Mary, trying to cheer him up.

"Not for this work, at least not officially. I'll be nominated in 1912, and pretty much every year after that, but it's too controversial and very hard to prove. I'm not sure they really understand it, to be honest. They'll eventually give it to me in 1921 for my work on light." He paused and flipped through the huge pile of papers on his desk. "Actually, I did that work this year too. It's here somewhere. Can you keep a secret? When they finally give me the Nobel Prize, I'm going to talk about relativity in my acceptance speech anyway." He chuckled. "That's going to really annoy a few people. Now – what do you know about time, young Mary?"

Mary looked at Barry. "I'm not sure anymore. I used to think it was just about seconds and minutes and hours and days and years, all clicking past and disappearing forever. But now I'm not sure. Time is more complicated than I thought."

Einstein beamed. "Correct! Did you know that the faster you move, the slower time travels? How

old did you say you were? Ten?"

Mary nodded.

"Imagine you left Earth today and travelled as fast as you could – say 99.5 per cent of the speed of light – for five years. For you! That's the important bit. It feels like five years to *you*. When you get back to Earth, how old will you be?"

"That's easy. I'll be fifteen."

"Exactly. But time ran slower for you, because of your motion, than for your friends back on Earth. For them, fifty years have passed. Imagine that. They'll all be wrinkled and old. Even older than Barry."

Mary frowned. "But that means I'll have travelled forward in time."

"Correct! Time travel into the future is easy. Well, it will be one day."

"And what about travelling to the past, like Barry and I just did? How does that work?"

Einstein gave Barry a worried look. "It's going to take a bigger brain than mine to work that out. But someone will do it . . . one day."

There was a loud knock at the door and a voice shouted, "Albert! Where are those patent applications? You should have finished them yesterday."

Einstein looked flustered. "You better leave. But you came for advice, didn't you? The best thing I can tell you is that you have time on your side. Some problems can't be figured out in a few weeks or months. Some take ten or twenty years. Yet, once you find the answer, it will be simple and beautiful. The universe loves simplicity. But we'll meet again, young Mary. You can count on that. Maybe in America. They're going to love me there. I'm going to be a *celebrity*!" To Mary's surprise, Einstein suddenly raised his eyebrows and poked his tongue out at her. "My face is going to be on T-shirts forever."

* * *

Albert Einstein was awarded the 1921 Nobel Prize in Physics 'for his services to theoretical physics, and especially for his discovery of the law of the photoelectric effect'. Pieces of his brain are still on display in two different American museums.

SPACE AND TIME

Einstein's theory of special relativity revolutionised the way we think about space and time. We now understand that the universe has three space dimensions – up/down, left/right and forward/backward – but also one time dimension. This is called the **space–time continuum**. To describe where an object is, we not only have to place it in space but also in time. Your book might be sitting on your desk now, but where will it be tomorrow?

In our world, time appears to be constant. You would have to travel incredibly fast before your time would slow down. But scientists now know that time slows dramatically when gravity is very strong, like at the edge of a black hole. If we could build a machine that let you sit next to a black hole, time would pass very slowly for you, but the rest of the universe would seem to be speeding up. When you moved away from the black hole, you would effectively have travelled forwards in time.

HOW FAST IS LIGHT?

A microwave heats food using energy waves that travel at the speed of light. In this experiment, you use a bar of chocolate to calculate how fast that is.

WHAT YOU NEED

· 1 plain chocolate bar (a flat one, without bumps or lumps or raised squares)
· Microwave
· Dinner plate
· Ruler with millimetres
· Calculator

WHAT TO DO

1. Find out what frequency your microwave uses. This information will be on a label inside the door, on the back or in the user manual. The frequency will be written either in megahertz (MHz) or gigahertz (GHz). Hertz is the number of times a wave goes up and down in 1 second.

2. Use the table below to convert your microwave's frequency to hertz.

Frequency (in GHz) _____ x 1,000,000,000

= _____ hertz

Frequency (in MHz) _____ x 1,000,000

= _____ hertz

3. If the microwave has a spinning plate on the bottom, take it out and put a normal dinner plate upside down in the microwave

4. Put the chocolate bar on the plate and heat it until it starts to melt in two or three places. This will take about 20 seconds.

5. Take the plate out and measure how far apart the melted spots of chocolate are. The distance between the melted spots of chocolate is half a wavelength.

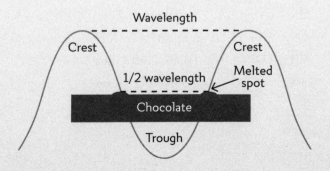

6. Use the formula below to calculate the wavelength in millimetres (mm).

Distance between melted chocolate (mm) _____ x 2

= _____ mm

7. Use the formula below to convert the wavelength to metres (m).

Wavelength (mm) _____ ÷ 1000 = _____ m

8. Use the formula below to calculate the speed of light in metres per second.

Speed of light = _____ x _____
                     frequency (hertz)   wavelength (m)

= _____ metres per second

WHAT TO LOOK FOR

The speed of light is approximately 300,000,000 (3×10^8) metres per second. How close was your answer?

3

A FAMILY AFFAIR

Marie Curie

*

Mary and Barry were back in the corridor of the research centre.

"How was that? Are you feeling all right?" asked Barry.

"Yes, I think so," said Mary. "A bit dizzy."

"Yes, well that's to be expected. Now, just let

me check my list." Barry pulled a scrap of paper out of his pocket and crossed out 'Albert Einstein'.

"Next we're visiting the first woman to win a Nobel Prize. She's also the first person to win two Nobels, and the only one to ever win for two different fields of science. Imagine that." Barry's voice trailed off, his eyes went glassy and there was a tiny smile on his face.

"Where are we going?" asked Mary loudly. Barry snapped to attention. "And when?" she continued. "Remember what Einstein said? You have to place us in space *and* in time."

"Paris. 1925."

He spun the dial and hit the button. The world around them went blurry for an instant and then they seemed to fall right into the middle of a large, light-filled room. Several wooden benches were laden with large glass jars with narrow tubes sticking out of them, Bunsen burners, old-fashioned scales, measuring jugs and machines that had so many dials and levers that Mary couldn't even guess what they might be for. The walls were lined with glass-fronted cabinets that were crammed full of books and papers. Except for one, which only held two small vials with handwritten labels. Mary peered at them. "Polonium. Radium." The second vial seemed to emit a faint blue glow, and she leaned in closer to get a better look.

"Away! Get away from that!" said Barry, jerking her a bit too hard by her arm.

Mary was about to get annoyed when a woman with slightly untamed grey frizzy hair and dressed in a very worn dark blue dress marched through the door. "Hurry up, Iréne," she demanded, looking behind her. "We've got work to do." A younger woman with similar, but darker, hair followed her into the lab.

Barry cleared his throat and the older woman gave him a stern stare. "Yes, Professor Marshall? What is it this time? I am extremely busy. I may already have my *two* Nobels, but that doesn't mean the work stops."

"My apologies, Madame Curie. But I've brought Mary to meet you, as we agreed. Mary, this is Madame Marie Curie and her daught—"

"Iréne," said the younger woman, putting out her hand for Mary to shake. "My name is Iréne." She looked closely at Mary. "She is very young, Mama."

"One is never too young to embark on a life of discovery," said Curie. "You should know that, Iréne. You began your scientific education when you were still a child. If it hadn't been for that unfortunate war, you would have had your doctorate years ago. Although you were very useful to me on the front, helping those poor young men with their terrible injuries."

"Congratulations, on the doctorate, Iréne," said Barry. "That was nice work you did on polonium."

Iréne blushed. "Thank you. I enjoyed it. And I'm teaching Mama's assistant, Frédéric, my techniques. In a few years, we will also win a Nobel—"

"Polonium was actually my discovery, Mary," interrupted Marie. "My husband Pierre helped – he built a nice piece of equipment that was very useful for measuring electrical activity in the air – but the idea! The idea was mine!"

"You shared the prize with him, Mama," said Iréne.

"Yes, yes. The first one. Not the second."

"What is polonium?" asked Mary.

"A radioactive element, my dear," said Marie, looking at her kindly for the first time. "A substance that emits energy from its core. From the atoms themselves! Imagine it! The other scientists were all obsessed with the first X-rays, peering at pictures of the bones inside people's bodies. X-rays are very useful, of course – I built mobile X-ray machines and used them to treat soldiers on the battlefields – but they have their limitations. The others knew about radiation, but they believed it to be a weaker force. They were wrong about that. It took Pierre and I several years to isolate the ultimate source of the energy we were measuring. We had to process tons of uranium before we finally found it. It turned out that these elements were so powerful that they only existed in the tiniest amounts in the minerals we were working with. In fact if they weren't radioactive, we wouldn't even have known they were there. We worked in an abandoned shed next to Pierre's school, night and day, through freezing winters. But we eventually succeeded. The first element, polonium, I named after my beloved homeland, Poland. The second we named radium, for its rays of energy. And do you know the most exciting part of all, Mary? We discovered that radiation can work magic inside the body. It can even kill cancer cells!"

"But isn't radiation dangerous?" asked Mary, looking worriedly at the glowing vials in the glass cabinet that had so interested her earlier.

Marie waved her hand dismissively. "Perhaps a little. But we all have to die sometime."

"Poor Papa," said Iréne. "I'm sure he was thinking about his work when he slipped under that horse-drawn cart. He was so tired. You were both so tired all the time. You still are, Mama."

Marie did look quite pale and thin, Mary noticed. In fact, so did Iréne. Mary edged further away from the glass cabinet.

"Yes, well, we mustn't keep you too long," said Barry, seeming eager to move on. "Do you have any advice for Mary?"

"You must love what you do, my dear. It takes time and single-minded dedication, this work of ours. I am the first woman to win a Nobel Prize, you know. It was not easy. But I loved my husband very much, and we both loved our work." She tugged at her dress. "This was my wedding dress. It is also my laboratory gown. You cannot be motivated by fame or riches. My children suffered. I was so busy all the time. I could have stopped toiling and made a fortune from my discoveries many years ago, but I chose to continue my research. And now my radiation therapy brings benefits for the whole of humanity."

"Excellent," said Barry. "Come on now, Mary, we must be off. There's no time to waste." He glanced nervously at the cabinet and its glass vials.

"What's the rush?" asked Mary. "Surely with the machine, we have all the time we need."

"No, we must go now," Barry replied, fumbling hurriedly with the time machine's dial.

Iréne grabbed hold of Mary's arm and whispered in her ear. "Be very careful, Mary. Sometimes our work can bring us great things – recognition, rewards, even love if you are as lucky as Mama and I have been. But we work right at the edge of what is known and what is not. And the unknown can be very dangerous."

The world tilted, and the two women became even thinner and paler before disappearing altogether.

Marie and Pierre Curie were awarded the 1903 Nobel Prize in Physics 'in recognition of the extraordinary services they have rendered by their joint researches on the radiation phenomena'. Marie Curie was also awarded the Nobel Prize in Chemistry 1911. Marie and Iréne both died from diseases caused by exposure to radiation.

DOUBLING UP

Marie Curie was the first person to win two Nobel Prizes but she wasn't the last. The work of John Bardeen (Physics, 1956 and 1972) helped to give the world electrical devices like radio, television, computers and mobile phones. Frederick Sanger (Chemistry, 1958 and 1980) described the exact structure of insulin, the hormone used to treat diabetes. His later work on DNA was an important step towards our understanding of the genes that make us human. Linus Pauling (Chemistry, 1954 and Peace, 1962) won his first Nobel for research into chemical bonds and his second for his work towards a ban on nuclear weapons tests.

Between them, Marie Curie's family won five Nobel prizes. Irène Curie shared the 1935 Nobel Prize in Chemistry with her husband, Frédéric Joliot-Curie. Marie's younger daughter, Ève, once joked that she was the only member of her family not to win one. However, Ève's husband was the director of UNICEF when it won the Nobel Peace Prize in 1965.

RADIATION AND PLANTS

Marie Curie won her Nobel Prize for her work on radiation. Light, heat and microwaves are all forms of radiation. In this experiment, you are going to see if the radiation from a microwave oven affects a seed and how it grows.

WHAT YOU NEED

- 12 seeds (choose a fast-growing plant like zucchini, radish, sunflower, lettuce, marigold, chives or basil)
- Potting mix
- Egg carton
- Paper towel
- Microwave oven
- Felt tip pen

WHAT TO DO

1. Fill all 12 cups of the egg carton with potting mix.
2. Mark 6 of the cups with a cross.

3. Plant 6 seeds in the unmarked cups (one seed per cup).

4. Put the other 6 seeds on a paper towel and microwave them for 5 seconds.

5. Plant the 6 microwaved seeds in the 6 cups marked with a cross.

6. Water the seeds (just a little bit).

7. Put the egg carton in a warm, sunny place. Water it lightly every day to keep the soil damp.

8. Take pictures of the egg carton every day. Make sure that you can see the crosses in your photographs.

WHAT TO LOOK FOR

Was there any difference in how quickly the seeds grew? Did the microwaved seeds grow faster or slower than the others? Did they grow at all?

4

AN AGE OF MARVELS

Guglielmo Marconi

Mary and Barry were in the middle of a crowded city street. Although it was dark and seemed very late, thousands of people were gathered outside a large sandstone building. Mary peered through the crowd at the steps and the columns and the tall tower with a clock on top and thought the building looked very familiar.

"Is this Sydney?" she asked.

"It shouldn't be," said Barry, fiddling with the dial on the time machine. "Oh, I know what's gone wrong. We're at the wrong end of the signal, that's all."

A man was standing on the steps of the Sydney Town Hall, making a speech in complete darkness. Mary caught something about a 'radio exhibition' and 'Italy', when the building behind him suddenly lit up. The man seemed startled and the lady standing next to Mary gasped. "Oh, my lord. Would you look at that! It's like magic."

The crowd cheered and applauded wildly.

"What's going on? Why is everyone clapping?" asked Mary.

"It's wireless, lovey," said the lady. "Those lights were just turned on by someone on the other side of the world." Barry pressed a button and the world tipped again.

"Sorry about that," said Barry. "I got the date right – 26 March 1930. We were just in the wrong place."

"I think we still might be," said Mary, leaning over a white metal railing to look down at the water. "We're on a boat. I don't really like boats, to be honest."

"She's a yacht, my dear," said a very tall, stern looking man who was climbing a set of stairs to the wooden deck where Barry and Mary were standing. He was wearing a neat black suit with a white handkerchief peeking out of the breast pocket, shiny black shoes and a flat white hat with a stiff black peak. "Her name is *Elettra*. And I am her captain." He put out his hand. "Guglielmo Marconi. And this is my wife, Maria." He held out his hand to a woman who had followed him very slowly up the stairs.

Mary looked at her in disbelief. She had a dead fox wrapped around her neck.

Barry nudged her. "Stop staring. Clothes were different in 1930." He shook Marconi's hand. "We actually stopped off in Sydney on our way here. The signal worked a treat."

"Yes, it was a great achievement," said Marconi. "An electrical impulse beamed from the *Elettra* in Genoa Harbour, Italy, 22,000 kilometres around the world in one-seventh of a second to turn on 2800 lights. I must apologise to the organisers, though. I got a bit overexcited and hit the switch a few minutes early."

"Is that what you won the Nobel Prize for," asked Mary. "Turning on those lights?"

"No, they gave me that twenty years ago," said Marconi. "When I was a young man, doing my early work on wireless radio signals. Everyone said it couldn't be done. Because the Earth is curved, they thought the signals would travel in a straight line and disappear into the sky. It was thought that the furthest a signal could travel was 300 kilometres. But they were wrong. Radio waves follow the shape of the Earth. In 1901 I sent a message from

England, 3200 kilometres across the Atlantic Ocean, to Canada.

"What did the message say?" asked Mary.

Marconi looked annoyed. "It doesn't matter what it said."

"But what was it?"

"S."

"S?"

"It was in Morse code. Dot. Dot. Dot. But that's not the important part. The point is that it showed that we could send messages between two places on the planet. That is particularly important for you Australians. Cut off from the rest of the world by oceans. All that empty space between your towns. In fact, that's why I chose Sydney for my demonstration. Which reminds me, I must write the speech I am delivering to the people of Sydney in a few days. Come below and see my office," said Marconi.

He ushered them down the stairs, along a short corridor and into a room that was almost entirely filled by machines made of levers, metal handles, dials, large round gauges with quivering needles and strange, squat, ridged tubes that sat underneath shining silver boxes with brass tubes coming out of them. Everything gleamed. It looked as if the whole room was polished every single day.

"The money my work has earned me has allowed me to turn *Elettra* into a floating laboratory. Here I can be independent and hide from curious eyes and distractions. I can work at all hours of the day or night and sail to places to do experiments that would be too hard to carry out on land. We live on *Elettra* too, don't we dear?" he added. Maria's eyes were closed, but she nodded. Mary thought she looked a bit pale and clammy.

"I have always loved to sail. In fact, when I began my work my greatest concern was for safety at sea. I realised that wireless transmission would allow ships to send and receive messages for the first time. And then a terrible day arrived – 14 April 1912. I had been offered a berth on the *Titanic*, you know, but I decided to sail to America a few days earlier. I was in New York when the news arrived that the *Titanic* had hit an iceberg and 1503 lives had been lost. But 712 people were saved, thanks to the distress calls from my company's wireless equipment that was on board." He picked up a gold plaque. "The survivors presented me with this. It is my most treasured possession. But that is in the past now. Today's experiment was about the future. We are living in an age of marvels. Imagine it, Mary, if you can. A world with no electric wires. Signals sent through the air from anywhere on planet, in any direction, uninterrupted by mountains or oceans. Even to space itself!"

"Sure. Like radio and television. And mobile phones and satellites and the rovers that landed on Mars and sent pictures back to Earth."

"Mary! Don't forget the rules. Not too much talk about the future," whispered Barry.

Marconi wobbled a little and grasped the nearest bench to steady himself. "Well, I had heard rumours from the others in the group, but they are indeed marvels."

"Do you have any advice for Mary, Mr Marconi?" asked Barry.

"You must seek out people who understand what you are trying to achieve. I am a proud Italian but when I wrote to Rome explaining my idea for a wireless telegraph machine they stamped my letter 'To the insane asylum' and never replied. So I went to England, where the customs officer called the Admiralty himself when he saw the equipment I had in my case. It was in England that I registered my first patent, set up my first company and did my most important work."

Maria interrupted. "I'm feeling rather unwell, Guglielmo. I think I need to rest."

As she turned to leave, Mary caught a glimpse

of a large bump underneath her long, black coat. "Congratulations!" she said.

Marconi smiled. "If the baby is a girl, we will call her Elettra."

"After your boat?" asked Mary.

"Of course. She is the greatest love of my life."

✳ ✳ ✳

The 1909 Nobel Prize in Physics was awarded to Guglielmo Marconi for his contribution to the development of wireless telegraphy. When he died in 1937, wireless stations fell silent for two minutes as a tribute to his life and his work.

RICH REWARDS

Marconi was born into a wealthy family, but his inventions made him even richer. He patented his first wireless transmitter in 1897. A patent is a legal document that gives someone the exclusive rights to an invention. It meant that only Marconi could make and sell his transmitters. Alfred Nobel himself patented his inventions from his work on explosives, including dynamite, a safe detonating cap and gunpowder. The fortune that he used to establish the Nobel Prize was made from these inventions.

Other Nobel Prize winners decided not to patent their discoveries. Wilhelm Röntgen, who discovered X-rays, said that his "inventions and discoveries belong to the world at large". Alexander Fleming did not patent penicillin, because he wanted to make sure that it was freely available to as much of the world's population as possible. For the same reason, Rosalyn Yalow did not patent her method of screening blood for diseases.

MORSE CODE

More than a century ago, Guglielmo Marconi sent a wireless message across a distance of 3200 kilometres using Morse code. Morse code uses different combinations of dots and dashes to represent letters, numbers and symbols. The decision about which combination of dots and dashes to use for each letter was based on how often each letter is used in the English language. The most commonly used letter – E – is represented by a single dot.

You can use Morse code to send your own messages.

THINGS TO LOOK FOR

There are lots of ways to use Morse code. You and a friend could use torches to send each other messages at night, or send messages silently by blinking quickly for a dot and blinking slowly for a dash. (Two students once used this method to cheat on a test.) Text your friend .-.. --- .-.. instead of LOL. You could even make a necklace with your name in Morse code.

There are lots of apps that help you learn, practise, send and receive Morse code messages.

WHAT TO DO

Character	Morse code	Character	Morse code	Character	Morse code
A	. -	N	-.	1	.----
B	-...	O	---	2	..---
C	-.-.	P	.--.	3	...--
D	-..	Q	--.-	4	....-
E	.	R	.-.	5	.....
F	..-.	S	...	6	-....
G	--.	T	-	7	--...
H	....	U	..-	8	---..
I	..	V	...-	9	----.
J	.---	W	.--	0	-----
K	-.-	X	-..-	Period	.-.-.-
L	.-..	Y	-.--	?	..--..
M	--	Z	--..	Comma	--..--

Use the table above to work out the Morse code for the international distress symbol SOS.

Character		S	O	S
Morse code		_____	_____	_____

Use the table to work out what this word is.

Morse code	..	-.	-	.	.-.	-.	.	-
Character	__	__	__	__	__	__	__	__

Write your own message in Morse code and send it to a friend.

Character	__	__	__	__	__	__	__	__
Morse code	__	__	__	__	__	__	__	__

Character	__	__	__	__	__	__	__	__
Morse code	__	__	__	__	__	__	__	__

Character	__	__	__	__	__	__	__	__
Morse code	__	__	__	__	__	__	__	__

Character	__	__	__	__	__	__	__	__
Morse code	__	__	__	__	__	__	__	__

Character	__	__	__	__	__	__	__	__
Morse code	__	__	__	__	__	__	__	__

You can google 'Morse code sound' to hear what it sounds like.

You can make a Morse code transmitter out of wire and a battery. It was the first electric gadget I ever built. Search for 'how to build a simple telegraph set' online. I liked the one made from a tin can, nails, wood, insulated wire and two AA batteries. My first attempt failed because I did not use insulated wire. Can you figure out why the wire needs to be insulated (plastic-coated)?

5

THE SECRET OF LIFE

Francis Crick, James Watson and Maurice Wilkins

"Where are we now?" asked Mary. They were in an outdoor quadrangle that was surrounded on all four sides by tall stone buildings with arched windows.

Barry looked around him. "King's College, London, in England. It's 1953, and we're here to meet the people who discovered what DNA looks like and how it works. Do you know what DNA is?"

Mary thought for a while. "It's something to do with genetics. Like, why I have blue eyes like my dad's."

"Correct. Genes are actually just tiny sections of DNA, which you have in every cell of your body. DNA is so small that no one knew what it actually looked like. Until these people came along. Come on. Let's get to the lab. They're waiting for us."

Mary followed Barry across the quadrangle. He pushed open a heavy wooden door to reveal four people standing in a very messy workshop.

Barry introduced her to two tall, skinny men. "Mary, this is Francis Crick and James Watson. They've been friends since they met at university—"

"Cambridge University," interrupted Francis, the older and balder of the two men. "Not this one. We've just popped over here to London to meet you."

"Francis and James have been puzzling over the structure of DNA for ages," said Barry.

"We've been trying to build a model from these," said James, who was American. He pointed at what looked like a large pile of rubbish scattered on a wooden bench. She tilted her head, trying to make some sense out of it.

"They didn't really help much," admitted Francis. "But this one is promising." He ushered Mary over to a large, flimsy model that was taller than Barry that was made out of hexagonal pieces of metal strung together with thin brass rods. It looked like a bit like a spiral staircase. She tilted her head to see if it made more sense sideways. It didn't.

"And this is Maurice Wilkins," continued Barry, indicating the third man. Mary thought the three men looked as if they could be brothers. She wondered if their DNA all looked the same too. "Maurice is a physicist and a biologist and he took the first X-ray photographs of DNA."

"I met James in Italy a few years ago," said Maurice. "I showed him my photos and the three of us have been working on the puzzle of DNA ever since. Oh, and this is my assistant, Rosalind Franklin," said Maurice, waving his hand dismissively at the very serious-looking woman standing behind him.

"No, I'm not," Rosalind said.

"Not what?" asked Maurice.

"I'm not your assistant," said Rosalind. "I've got a PhD in physical chemistry from Cambridge University and I've already published five papers. I'm also trying to figure out what DNA looks like. I take X-ray photographs too, but mine are better than Maurice's. It's called X-ray crystallography."

"But ... you're a wo—" Maurice stopped talking as Rosalind shot him a stern glance.

"I'm a what? Expert in my field? Pioneer?" she said.

"Exactly what I was going to say," interrupted Barry, sensing an argument in the air. "So, these four are just about to work out that, up close, DNA looks a bit like a twisted ladder. It has two long strands that wind around each other. They're going to call it a 'double helix'."

"OK ..." said Mary, thinking that it didn't really sound very exciting.

"It's a very important discovery!" said Francis. "It means that we know how all the cells in your body multiply and grow, but still have the exact same DNA. Think of it like a zipper. Each piece of the zip – each tooth – has to be exactly the right place for your zip to do up properly, right?"

"Yes, I guess so," said Mary, looking down at the zip on her jacket.

"Well, the double helix shape works a bit like that. But now imagine that the teeth on your zips are made up of four slightly different shapes. Each pair on either side of the zip has to be perfectly matched for the zip to work. The DNA unzips as the cell divides, and then each single strand has to build a matching strand so it can zip up again properly. That's how one double helix of DNA can unzip, and then create two DNA molecules that are identical to each other. Brilliant, isn't it?" Francis beamed at Mary. "It's a very beautiful structure," he added. "I don't like to brag, but we've basically discovered the secret of life."

"How did you work all that out?" asked Mary.

"Oh, Maurice showed us his X-rays," said James.

Rosalind cleared her throat loudly.

"Ah, yes. And he also gave us some of Rosalind's X-ray photographs to look at. Excellent images. Particularly the one called 'Photo 51'. It really showed the shape. It was the last piece that we needed to solve the puzzle. We were very lucky," added Francis quickly.

"Nobody asked me if you could look at my photos," muttered Rosalind, looking annoyed.

"Sorry about that, Rosalind," said James, looking uncomfortable.

"So, all four of you are going to share the Nobel Prize! That's nice," said Mary.

The three men shifted uneasily. "Not exactly," mumbled Maurice.

"Not me," stated Rosalind. "One thing we didn't know was that X-rays aren't exactly great for you. And I spent most of my life working with them, which was not good for my health. In fact ..." She paused. "I'm not supposed to know this, but Einstein has a big mouth. I'm going to die in a few years. Nine years from now, these three will win the Nobel Prize. But I'll be dead."

Mary thought Rosalind looked very cross about that. Fair enough, she thought.

"Unfortunately, the Nobel Prize can only be awarded to people who are alive," Barry said hurriedly. "Well, they made an exception for Ralph Steinman in 2011, but he only died a few days before the announcement and the committee didn't know ..." His voice trailed off as he realised Rosalind was staring at him with a very odd expression on her face.

"I tried," said James, looking anxiously at Rosalind. "I did ask them to give you one too. And

I thanked you in my book."

Rosalind pressed her lips together. It wasn't quite a smile.

"Yes. In the epilogue. Right at the back. Thanks for that."

There was an uncomfortable silence for a few moments.

"Anyway," said Barry brightly, trying to lighten the mood. "Any advice for Mary?"

"Don't die," muttered Rosalind.

"Collaboration," said Francis. "It took everyone in this room to work it out. None of us could have done it on our own. And don't underestimate people who seem quite different to you. You never know – they could have the final key to the puzzle."

Rosalind Franklin died in April 1958 of ovarian cancer. She was 37 years old. Francis Crick, James Watson and Maurice Wilkins were awarded the 1962 Nobel Prize in Physiology or Medicine 'for their discoveries concerning the molecular structure of nucleic acids and its significance for information transfer in living material'.

UNSUNG HEROES

Rosalind Franklin is not the only person to have missed out on a Nobel Prize for work done in collaboration with other scientists.

Jocelyn Bell was an astrophysics graduate student who found strange signals coming from the stars. They turned out to be pulsars – rotating neutron stars. Her supervisor, Anthony Hewish (Physics, 1974) was awarded the Nobel Prize for his work on pulsars.

Nikola Tesla was an inventor, electrical engineer, mechanical engineer, physicist and futurist. He made many important discoveries and his work was the basis of the electrical networks that distribute power to our homes and businesses. There is a rumour that the 1915 prize for Physics was to be awarded jointly to Tesla and Thomas Edison but, because of their fierce rivalry, both men refused to share the prize. Neither of them ever won.

Douglas Prasher was part of the team that developed green fluorescent protein. They did their work in 1992, but by the time they won the Chemistry prize in 2008, Prasher had given up science and was working as a bus driver.

EXTRACT DNA FROM A STRAWBERRY

Because DNA is so small, you can't usually see it without powerful microscopes. But every strawberry cell has eight copies of the strawberry's DNA, instead of just one. That means you can collect lots of DNA at once. There is so much DNA that you can see it without a microscope.

WHAT YOU NEED

- 1 strawberry
- 30 ml dishwashing liquid
- 1 teaspoon salt
- Medicine dropper
- Ice-cold methylated spirits (or rubbing alcohol or ethanol)
- Zip lock plastic bag
- Plastic cup
- Gauze
- Rubber band
- Test tube (or specimen jar)
- Wooden skewer

1. Wash the strawberry and take off the leaves.

2. Mix the dishwashing liquid and salt with 500ml water. This is the DNA extracting solution.

3. Put the strawberry into the zip lock bag with 2 tablespoons of the DNA extracting solution. Seal the bag tightly and make sure there aren't any air bubbles.

4. Crush the strawberry gently through the bag.

5. Put the gauze over the opening of the plastic cup and secure it with the rubber band.

6. Pour the strawberry solution gently into the cup through the gauze.

7. Fill the medicine dropper with strawberry solution from the cup and squirt it into the test tube.

8. Add a full dropper of the cold alcohol to the test tube. Be careful not to tilt or tip the test tube. You don't want the two liquids to mix.

9. Look carefully where at where the strawberry mixture and the alcohol meet. You should see a white thread-like cloud appearing here.

10. Keep the test tube still and gently twirl the wooden skewer in the white cloud.

The long threads that you can see clinging to the skewer are the strawberry's DNA molecules. The dishwashing liquid bursts open the cells of the strawberries, releasing the DNA. The DNA clumps together and become visible. DNA is not soluble in alcohol; therefore, it makes the DNA strands clump together and become visible to the naked eye.

6

THE MIRACLE CURE

Alexander Fleming

"It's cold," complained Mary, pulling her coat tightly around her. The room they were in was unheated and a chilly draft from an open window wasn't helping.

"Not really," said Barry. "It's actually the end of summer. Although it is England. This is probably about as warm as it gets. But I'll close this window for you."

"And it's very messy," she said. "Don't any of these famous scientists ever tidy up?"

Barry glanced at her. "You're a bit grumpy today. Are you feeling OK?"

"I'm fine." Mary sneezed violently and the dust on the table next to her went flying into the air, swirled in the beams of sunlight and settled gently back down on top of some flat, circular glass dishes that were scattered along a long wooden bench. "Where's your scientist?"

"He's been on holiday for a few weeks. He should be back soon."

The door burst open and a tall man with a long face and sticking out ears rushed in.

"Barry! Good to see you again. Oh, Mary, you don't look well. Sit down, sit down." He brushed a pile of papers off a chair, sat Mary down on it, then rummaged in his pocket of his lab coat. "Would you like a sweetie? I think I had some peppermints in here."

"You don't sound English," she said accusingly.

"Who told you I was English?" the man asked her. "I'm Scottish. I'm actually going to be one of the most famous Scots ever. Anyway, I'm also a doctor and you look sick to me."

"I'm fine," repeated Mary crossly. "But you need to clean your lab."

The man laughed loudly and Barry chuckled along with him. Mary glared at them both.

"Sorry, Mary," said Barry. "But this is Sir—"

"I'm not a 'sir' yet. Don't jump the gun!"

"Sorry. This is Alexander Fleming. And this mess is the reason he is about to make a discovery that will change medicine forever."

"I suppose I should throw these away," said Fleming as he sorted through the pile of glass dishes. "Wait a minute. That's funny. Come over here and have a look, Barry. I know how much you like getting up close with bacteria."

Barry frowned. "I have no idea what you are talking about. Ignore him, Mary."

Fleming and Barry huddled over one of the dishes. Mary shuffled over to see what all the fuss was about.

"Eeewww," she said. "It's gone all mouldy. Did you leave the lid off?"

"That's not all mould," Fleming said. "The small white spots all over these petri dishes are bacteria. I've been growing it on purpose. But I think this one must have been contaminated. In fact, you're right. The furry green stuff *is* some kind of mould. I must have left the lid off and it floated in while I was on holiday. I don't know where it could have come from, though. It's not as if I left a window open."

Barry smiled at Mary from behind Fleming's back and gave her a thumbs up.

"What do you notice about the bacteria?" continued Fleming.

Mary looked more closely. "There aren't any spots near the fur."

"Correct. I think the mould has killed it all. Or at least stopped it from growing. Do you know what this means?" Fleming was starting to sound excited. "It means I've just stumbled on a way to kill bacteria."

"Is that good?" asked Mary.

"Good? It's fantastic! I have been trying to find a way to defeat bacteria since I was a doctor during the war, working in the battlefield hospitals in France."

"Oh, did you meet Madame Curie and her daughter there? They were doing X-rays."

"No, I don't think so. It was a busy place. Many of the soldiers I treated didn't die from their wounds – at least not immediately. They lingered and the wounds got infected and they died slow, painful deaths from the infection. We tried treating them with antiseptics, but that seemed to make them worse, not better. I'll never forget the sight of all that pus. And the stinky smell of the gangrene."

Mary wobbled a little and sat back down. "I think I might be a bit sick, actually. But congratulations."

"Nature made it. I just found it. And there's lots of work still to do. It's going to be very hard to isolate the active ingredient in the mould. It's penicillin – one of the most commonly used antibiotics. But you need lots and lots of the mould to make enough of it to help someone get better."

Barry chimed in. "And that won't happen for a while yet. Not until a scientist called Howard

Florey – he's Australian, by the way – and Ernst Chain get to work on it. That won't be for more than ten years but, once they start, things are going to move quickly. By 1944 they will be mass producing penicillin. They're going to make enough to treat all the soldiers wounded in World War II."

"Another world war?" said Fleming quietly. "Dear me."

"Oops," said Barry. "I didn't mean to say that. But Mary, this is the exact moment that modern medicine was born. Penicillin has saved millions of lives all over the world."

Fleming blushed. "Not bad for an accidental discovery. I certainly didn't plan to revolutionise medicine. But I guess that's exactly what I've done."

Barry checked his watch. "We better leave you to it, Alexander. Do you have any advice for Mary?"

"Get yourself to a doctor, young lady. I think you have a nasty cold coming on."

"I suppose I'm going to need your antibiotics," said Mary.

"No! Absolutely not. You mustn't ever use them unless you have to. And you mustn't ever use too little of them, or stop taking them before all the bacteria have been killed. They're tricky things, bacteria. They can get used to anything. In the future, if you aren't careful, the bugs will all end up resistant to antibiotics and then your world will be like ours has been all this time. I sincerely hope that evil can be averted. And all that pus and gangrene."

Mary's head swam and she nearly slid off the chair.

"Actually, I meant do you have advice about winning the Nobel Prize," said Barry.

"Ah! In that case, never neglect something that looks extraordinary. It's probably a false alarm, but it might just be the clue that will lead you to an important discovery."

✳ ✳ ✳

The Nobel Prize in Physiology or Medicine 1945 was awarded jointly to Sir Alexander Fleming, Ernst Boris Chain and Sir Howard Walter Florey 'for the discovery of penicillin and its curative effect in various infectious diseases'.

ACCIDENTAL DISCOVERIES

Fleming is not the only person to win a Nobel Prize as the result of a fortunate accident. In 1965, astronomers Arno Penzias and Robert Wilson were working on a giant antenna. They were annoyed about a persistent background noise that they thought was caused by pigeon poo on their antenna. Eventually, after lots of cleaning, they realised they were picking up leftover radiation from the Big Bang that created the universe. It won them the 1978 Nobel Prize in Physics.

The very first Nobel Prize in Physics went to Wilhelm Röntgen in 1901 for his accidental discovery of X-rays. He was studying electron beams in a vacuum tube when he noticed that a nearby fluorescent screen was glowing. He had found an invisible form of radiation that could travel through cardboard – and human flesh. He tested his discovery by X-raying his wife's hand (she was spooked by seeing her own skeleton!).

SPOILING FAST FOOD

Alexander Fleming only made his discovery because mould grew in his uncovered petri dishes. This experiment shows how mould grows on food under different conditions.

WHAT YOU NEED

- 8 glass jars with lids
- Tongs or disposable gloves
- 4 hamburgers from 4 different fast-food chains
- 4 serves of chips or fries from 4 different fast-food chains
- Permanent marker
- Camera

WHAT TO DO

1. Wash the glass jars with hot soapy water and rinse thoroughly

2. Place jars in a pot of boiling water for a few minutes to sterilise them. This removes any mould spores. After this step, only touch the jars with tongs or using disposable gloves.

3. Buy the hamburgers and chips or fries. When they have cooled down, place them in the labelled glass jars. Label the jars with the name of the fast-food chain.

4. Take a photo of each jar at the same time every day.

WHAT TO LOOK FOR

Some fast-food chains use natural chemicals in their burgers to keep them fresher for longer. Mould needs three things to grow: mould spores, moisture and food.

If the chips were cooked in very hot oil, this might have killed the spores.

Because the jars are sealed, the hamburgers and fries only have the moisture they went in with. Were they dry to start with?

Mould loves to eat sugar. How much sugar was in the food? Salt stops mould from growing. How salty was the food?

Which jar do you think will have the most mould after a few days? Which do you think will have the least? What do your photos show?

Is all of your food mouldy? You might see lots of different coloured moulds growing on the burgers. It might be yellow, white, green, red or black.

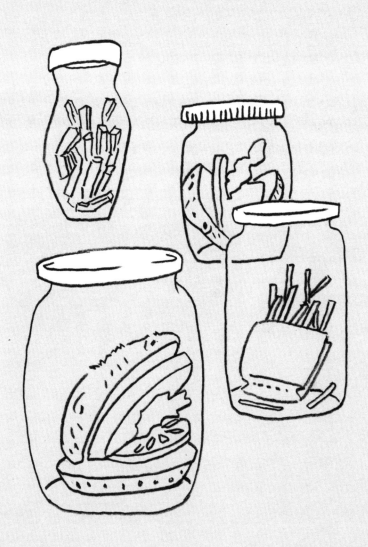

After penicillin, many other antibiotics were discovered to be produced by moulds and bacteria. Why should that be? Well, bacteria in the soil and environment are all competing against each other for their nutrition and space to grow. Over millions of years they developed special chemicals (antibiotics) that could poison other bacteria and organisms – or digest plant matter to help them survive. So it's not surprising that we found lots of new antibiotics from different bacteria, not just penicillin mould.

7

EVERYTHING OLD IS NEW AGAIN

Tu Youyou

Mary picked herself up, feeling quite dizzy. She wasn't sure if it was Fleming's talk about pus and gangrene or the constant whirling and spinning that time travel seemed to involve, but she was starting to find it all a bit unpleasant. She looked around. She and Barry were in the middle of a concrete courtyard, in front of a very wide white building with huge red Chinese lettering on top of it.

"Where's this?" she asked.

"The Institute of Chinese Materia Medica in Beijing, the capital city of China," said Barry. "But we better not hang around too long. It's 1972 and there aren't many Westerners here at the moment. We're going to stick out like sore thumbs."

Barry hurried Mary down a long hallway until they reached a door with a sign that simply said "Project 523".

"In here," he said, pushing the door open to reveal a laboratory that, as well as being full of the usual equipment that Mary was used to seeing – long benches crammed full of glass tubes clamped to beakers and jugs of all shapes and sizes, Bunsen burners, bottles and jars containing mysterious substances and paper covered in scribbled handwriting – also had a pile of what looked like dried grass on a central table. A woman with short black hair and sensible glasses was carefully sorting through the leaves.

Barry cleared his throat. "Excuse me, Mrs Tu. We'd like to talk to you about your research."

The woman bowed and then looked up at them and smiled. "Welcome, Professor Marshall. Thank you for visiting. I have much to show you and your young friend."

"Mary, this is Tu Youyou. She's working on a top-secret project for the Chinese government. They've asked her to search through ancient books about herbal medicines to find a cure for malaria."

"What's malaria?" asked Mary.

"It is a terrible disease," said Tu. "It is carried by mosquitoes and makes people very sick with fevers, vomiting and painful headaches. Every year, many people die. Especially the young and the old and the poor. But I think we have found something that might help." Tu picked up a handful of the dried leaves. "This is *quinghao* (pronounced 'ching how'). In the West, you call it sweet wormwood. Here, smell." She handed it to Mary.

Mary sniffed the leaves. "It smells a bit like mint, but ... mustier."

Tu smiled. "Chinese people have always used it to treat the fevers that come and go during the tropical wet season and cause much sickness. We believe that these are caused by malaria, so we have been trying to work out what this herb contains that makes it so effective. I think we may have succeeded, but it took a long time. To begin with we boiled the leaves, as we do with most traditional Chinese herbs, but the medicine did not work as well as we hoped. So we went back to a text called *Emergency Prescriptions Kept Up One's Sleeve* that was written more than 1600 years ago. We quickly realised our mistake. The recipe simply said to soak a bunch of leaves in water and drink the juice. The heat from the boiling water had been killing the medicine. Our new preparation has worked well – none of the mice or monkeys have suffered. But we are running out of time, so last week we decided it was time for a trial on people." Tu paused, and glanced at Barry as if asking for permission to continue.

"And when you say 'people'," Barry encouraged her, "you mean ..."

Tu bowed her head. "I mean myself."

Mary was shocked. "You experimented on *yourself*? Are you allowed to do that? It sounds a bit dangerous to me."

"It is not unknown," Tu replied, glancing again at Barry. "Many scientists do it. Sometimes it is the only way to convince others that your theories are correct. And, as the head of this research group, it was my responsibility," She smiled at Mary. "Sadly, Miss Mary, the tea did not taste like mint. The people who have used it for centuries to treat fever call it 'bitter grass' and I now understand why. However, I have had no ill effects, so our superiors have allowed us to test the extract more widely. We have called it artemisinin."

"Mrs Tu, do you know how many lives you have saved?" asked Barry.

Tu shook her head. "I am aware that your contraption allows me to know the future, Mr Marshall, but I have no interest in that. I just wish to complete my task."

"More than 200 million people have received your medicine. That's millions of people who would have died without your work."

"*Our* work," Tu said. "I am just one of many on Project 523."

"But you were the one who discovered artemisinin, weren't you?" asked Mary.

Tu looked uncomfortable. "Miss Mary, in my culture we do not crave individual rewards. We work for the whole society. It is not important to receive applause."

"It wasn't until 2005 that anyone even worked out that Mrs Tu was the one that made the discovery," said Barry. "She left her children behind and travelled to an area of China where people suffered terribly from malaria, so she could see it for herself. She read thousands of traditional recipes and tested hundreds of extracts before she found artemisinin."

"It was important work," said Tu quietly. "I was willing to sacrifice my personal life. I saw many, many children die."

"The Chinese scientists tried to tell the rest of the world what they had found, but no one would listen," continued Barry. "It took more than twenty years before Western science finally paid attention and began to make enough artemisinin to treat people with malaria all over the planet. And it was only then that someone thought to ask who had made this incredible breakthrough. They had to go back and look through all the scientists' notebooks and read private letters and even records of secret meetings to work out that it was Mrs Tu."

Tu lowered her head again. "I do my work to thank my country for the education it has given me. I do not want fame."

"What *do* you want, Mrs Tu?" asked Mary.

"Miss Mary, I know you are here for advice," said Tu, looking intently at her. "Listen carefully. It is a scientist's responsibility to fight for the health of all humans. To receive awards is merely the icing on the cake. I feel more rewarded by hearing that so many patients have been cured." She bowed deeply. "Thank you both for your visit. But now I have important work to do."

Tu Youyou was awarded the 2015 Nobel Prize in Physiology or Medicine 'for her discoveries concerning a novel therapy against malaria'.

A WIN FOR EVERYONE

Alfred Nobel wrote in his will: "It is my express wish that in awarding the prizes no consideration be given to the nationality of the candidates, but that the most worthy shall receive the prize, whether he be Scandinavian or not." Very few women could be scientists back in 1895 so, although Nobel could imagine a scientist that wasn't Scandinavian, it probably didn't occur to him that 'he' could actually be a 'she'.

More than 100 years later, Tu Youyou became one of just eighteen female Nobel Prize winners in science. This was a huge achievement, especially as she was also the first Chinese scientist to win for medicine and the first Chinese woman to ever win a Nobel Prize.

The world has changed a lot since 1895. The talents and achievements of women and people from different cultures are now being recognised and celebrated. This is good news for everyone – just ask all those people who have benefitted from Tu's work on malaria.

NATURAL INSECT REPELLENT

Tu Youyou made her discovery by experimenting with natural remedies and everyday plants. You can use ingredients from plants to make your own insect repellent.

Warning: do not conduct this experiment in areas known to have mosquito-borne viruses.

Check with your parents or a teacher first.

WHAT YOU NEED

- Spray bottle
- 5ml (1 teaspoon) eucalyptus or citronella essential oil
- 1 tablespoon vodka (or rubbing alcohol)
- 150ml natural witch hazel
- 1 teaspoon of vegetable glycerin (optional)
- 150ml water (or vinegar)

WHAT TO DO

1. Place oil in the spray bottle.

2. Add vodka and shake.

3. Add witch hazel and shake.

4. Add glycerine, if you are using it. This helps the mixture stay combined.

5. Add water and shake again.

6. Shake before each use, because the oil and water will separate.

WHAT TO LOOK FOR

Test your insect repellent with a simple experiment. You will need to do this with a friend. One person sprays the repellent on their bare arms and the other one doesn't. Go outside just as it's getting dark (this is when mosquitoes appear). Do fewer mosquitos land on the person who has used the repellent?

You could also do this on your own by spraying repellent on just one arm.

8

WE ARE ALL MADE OF STARS

Subrahmanyan Chandrasekhar

"Oh, great. Another boat," said Mary. They were on the deck of a large cruise liner and although it was very dark she was pretty sure that this time they were nowhere near land. This really wasn't helping her queasy stomach.

"This is much bigger than Marconi's yacht," said Barry. "It's the same year though – 1930. Now, where is he?" Barry looked around and spotted a young man leaning on a railing, gazing up at the stars. "Subrahmanyan Chandrasekhar?"

The man looked over. "Barry! Yes, it's me. Sorry, I was miles away." He walked over to them and held out his hand. "Hello, Mary. Please, call me Chandra."

Mary shook his hand and studied him. He was much younger than the Nobel Prize winners Barry had introduced her to so far and, although he looked just as serious as the others had, there was a twinkle in his eye and a rebellious curl in his thick black hair.

"Where is this boat going?" she asked. "And are we nearly there?"

"No, we are sailing from India to England. I'm on my way to study at Cambridge University. It's a very long journey."

"Chandra got a scholarship," said Barry. "He's quite brilliant. And only nineteen. Basically a child prodigy." He sighed deeply.

Chandra laughed. "We're all young compared to the stars, Barry."

They all looked up at the sky. Mary gasped. She had never seen so many stars. They spread out above them like an infinite sparkling dome. She realised she was seeing more of the universe than had ever been revealed to her before. She felt tiny and insignificant and a little bit dizzy. "Beautiful, aren't they?" said Chandra. "Did you know that all the atoms on our planet, even the ones that the three of us are made of, were created inside stars like those? Stars have so much energy and their core is so dense that they squeeze hydrogen atoms together until the atoms themselves combine to form helium. Then the helium atoms fuse to make beryllium atoms, and it keeps going like that, all the way up the periodic table until atoms of iron are being made deep in the star's core. Then, in the final second of the star's life, it explodes. It's a huge explosion – bigger than millions of atomic bombs. It's called a supernova. And in this last second of life, the rest of the elements are created. Iron becomes gold, lead, copper and silver and the explosion scatters the atoms all through the universe. The star's death makes it possible for the universe, and life itself, to grow."

"And then is the star just … gone?" asked Mary.

"Oh, no. If it's small enough, what's left is a tiny, very dense, star. Imagine our Sun squashed down until it could fit into a city. But if the star is very big, its own gravity pulls in everything around it until it's all compressed into a point that's so small it has no volume. Nothing can escape. Not even light. Perhaps not even time, but I'm not sure about that – you'd have to check with Einstein."

"Will that happen to the Sun?" asked Mary nervously.

"No. I've been killing time on this journey by doing some maths. It turns out that our Sun isn't big enough to explode or collapse that way. It will just become a small hot star called a white dwarf. Not for about five billion years, though. No need to worry."

"He got the maths right about the biggest size a star has to be to turn into a white dwarf. It's called the Chandrasekhar Limit. And he basically just predicted the existence of black holes," Barry whispered in Mary's ear. "Great discovery, Chandra," he said loudly.

"I don't really think of it as a discovery. It just seems, in a strange way, as if it has always been there and I just happened to pick it up," said Chandra. "My uncle made his most famous discovery on a boat too, you know. His name is Chandrasekhara Venkata Raman. When he sailed to Europe in 1921, he wondered why the ice of glaciers and the water of the Mediterranean Sea were blue. He worked out that when light that travels through a transparent material, it changes wavelength. It's called the

Raman effect. They're giving him the Nobel Prize for Physics this year."

Chandra looked a bit gloomy for a minute. "My uncle only had to wait nine years. I'll have to wait more than fifty years for my Nobel Prize. No one is going to believe me. Not even Einstein himself. It's all perfectly clear in the maths, but even my best friend says it must be impossible. He thinks there must be some kind of unknown, special law of nature that stops a star from collapsing entirely until it has no volume. He said it was an absurd idea. The other scientists in Europe agreed with my calculations but none of them will publicly support my theory. In the end I'll even have to leave Europe and move to America. No one in England will employ me as a lecturer. I'm too controversial. Or maybe just too different."

"You'll keep yourself busy, though," said Barry, trying to cheer him up.

"Of course," Chandra smiled again. "I have a plan. Every ten years, I will dedicate myself to researching one important topic. I'll explore everything that I can about that subject, make contributions to our understanding of it, and write it all up. And then I'll move on to another topic. That should keep things interesting. Don't stand still too long, Mary. That's the trick."

"It helps if you're a genius," muttered Barry under his breath.

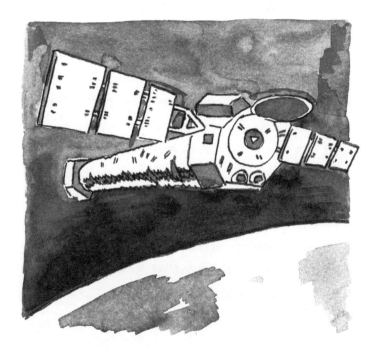

Chandra either didn't hear Barry or chose to ignore him. "And don't forget art! And music! And literature! I get the same thrill from a wonderfully carved sculpture as I do from a beautiful mathematical relationship. Art will make your lectures much more interesting to your students, but they will also help you to do science better. Science and beauty are not separate things. Look for the science in the beautiful things in nature that intrigue you the most."

"Like the stars," said Mary, looking up to the night sky again.

"Exactly," said Chandra softly. "Like the stars."

❋ ❋ ❋

The Nobel Prize in Physics 1983 was awarded to Subrahmanyan Chandrasekhar 'for his theoretical studies of the physical processes of importance to the structure and evolution of the stars'. Today, NASA's 'Chandra' observatory orbits the Earth, discovering new black holes.

THE LONG WAIT

Chandrasekhar was seventy-three years old when he was finally awarded the Nobel Prize for the work he began when he was just nineteen. The average time between a Nobel-worthy discovery and the scientist being awarded the prize is twenty years, but the delay is getting longer and longer every year.

Some people are worried that this time lag will mean that scientists could miss out on a Nobel Prize because, like Rosalind Franklin, they don't live long enough to win. The average age of a scientist winning a Nobel Prize is now sixty-eight.

However, the Nobel Committee believes it is important to wait for experimental proof of a discovery or theory before it awards a prize. Chandrasekhar's work, like that of many other theoretical physicists, was based on mathematics. It took a long time before it could be verified by an experiment or observation.

COUNTING STARS

Subrahmanyan Chandrasekhar was inspired to investigate the stars when he looked up at the night sky from a boat in the middle of the ocean. This experiment helps you understand the difference between how many stars you can see in the sky in different places.

WHAT YOU NEED

· Toilet roll tube
· Calculator

WHAT TO DO

1. Choose a night when there are no clouds in the sky. Go outside and write down all the light sources you can see (for example, street lights, shops, car headlights).

2. Keeping the tube still, look up at the sky. Count how many stars you can see through the tube. Do this 3 more times, looking at different parts of the sky each time.

3. Use the table below to record your observations and work out the average number of stars you saw.

Location 1: _____

Lifght Sources: _____

NUMBER OF STARS SEEN THROUGH TUBE

Observation 1: _____

Observation 2: _____

Observation 3: _____

Observation 4: _____

Average number of stars seen = _____
(Add the four numbers above and divide by 4)

4. Go to a different place that is darker (for example, a large park or somewhere further from the city). Repeat steps 1 and 2.

Location 2: _____

Lifght Sources: _____

NUMBER OF STARS SEEN THROUGH TUBE

Observation 1: _____

Observation 2: _____

Observation 3: _____

Observation 4: _____

Average number of stars seen = _____
(Add the four numbers above and divide by 4)

WHAT TO LOOK FOR

There are the same number of stars in the sky in both places. Why can you see more stars in one place than the other?

During the day, the sun is so bright that it outshines all the stars in the sky. Bright lights also make the sky brighter. The further we are from the cities and towns, the more stars we can see.

In 1994, an earthquake knocked out all the power to the American city of Los Angeles. Suddenly people could see thousands more stars than usual. Some people were so surprised that they called the local observatory to tell them that more stars had appeared in the sky.

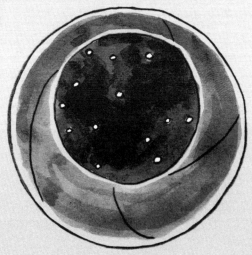

9

A LIFETIME'S WORK

Gertrude Elion

"Whoops," said Barry, frowning at the time machine. "Wrong time."

"Not again," groaned Mary. They were in a cemetery and a funeral was taking place just beside them. But at least they were back on solid ground, she thought.

"It's tricky, this time travel business," said Barry, stabbing frantically at the dial. "Sometimes the pull of a significant moment in someone's life interferes with where you've told the stupid thing you want to go."

"Is this a Nobel Prize winner's funeral?" asked Mary.

"No, they tend not to have very strong feelings about their own funerals. Probably because they don't actually go to them. Anyway, it's 1933 so she's still only fifteen. She won't die for ages and ages yet."

Mary peeked at the people who were starting to leave the funeral. A girl with thick wavy dark hair cut in a short bob was still standing beside the grave.

"Come on, Trudy," said a man in a long black coat that looked as if it had seen better days. "We have to leave now." He put his arm around her and walked her away from the grave. As they passed by, Mary looked curiously at the girl. She was crying, but underneath the tears there was a very determined look on her face.

"Father, nobody should ever suffer as much as Grandpa did."

"You're right, Trudy. It's a terrible thing,
cancer. But there is no treatment for it."

"I'm going to find one," said Trudy, wiping her
nose with the sleeve of a black cardigan that looked

too thin to protect her from the cold breeze that was rustling the autumn leaves loose from the trees. "And I want to start right away."

Her father shook his head. "You know we can't afford to send you to college."

"The women's college in New York offer the best students free tuition. I'm going to go there."

"Psst! Mary! I think I've fixed it," said Barry, beckoning at her from behind a tree. "Let's go. We're heading for 1998."

As the cemetery disappeared in a blur of grass and gravestones, Mary did the maths in her head. "But she'll be eighty by then. Couldn't we go a bit earli—"

But they were already standing at the back of a huge auditorium that was packed with people wearing black robes with colourful sashes and hats that looked like sheets of cardboard. Mary privately decided that everyone looked very stupid, as if they were dressed up as wizards.

Barry nudged her. "There she is."

An elderly woman walked slowly across the stage. People were applauding and cheering loudly. The woman accepted a roll of paper tied with a bright red ribbon and then turned to the crowd and waved it triumphantly in the air.

Mary was confused. "Is that her Nobel Prize?"

"No," said Barry. "She got that ten years ago. This is her honorary Doctor of Science from Harvard University. It's a bit like a PhD, but better."

"Can you win a Nobel Prize if you don't have a PhD?"

"Well, I did," said Barry. "Oxford University gave me an honorary Doctor of Science five years after I won the Nobel Prize. But this one is even more special than mine was, because

Gertrude Elion was never able to finish her university studies."

"Why not?"

"I'll let her tell you," said Barry, ushering Mary to the front of the auditorium and through a small door beside the stage.

The woman was lowering herself gently into an armchair. "Hello, Barry. I hope you don't mind if I sit down. I was standing up there for ages before it was finally my turn." She took off her hat, revealing wispy, bright orange hair that sprang up as it was released, revealing a very high forehead.

"Are you sure this is her?" Mary whispered to Barry. "She looks like a clown." Barry poked her quite hard in the back.

"It certainly is me," said Elion. "We all get old some day. Well, those of us who are lucky, anyway. And there's nothing wrong with my ears." She smiled at Mary, who was blushing so hard she felt as if her face might burst into flames.

"Mary is wondering why this is such a special day for you," said Barry.

"Oh, I don't care much about awards," said Elion. "Although this one does give me a lot of satisfaction. I spent years studying part-time for my PhD at night while I worked as a research assistant in a lab during the day, but my employer told me I had to choose between going to night school and my job. I chose my job. It was very hard to get, so I wasn't going to throw it away. When I got my Masters degree in Chemistry – I was the only woman in the class – I applied for fifteen fellowships. Guess how many I was offered, Mary?"

Mary thought for a moment. "Five?"

"Lower."

"Three?"

"None. Not one. Nobody took me seriously. They wondered why I wanted to be a chemist when no women were doing that. They had never had a woman in the laboratory before and they thought I would be 'a distracting influence'. I ended up going to secretarial college." Trudy snorted. "I only lasted six weeks. I managed to get a job in a food lab, testing pickles and mayonnaise, until eventually I began working as an assistant to George Hitchings. We worked together for the rest of his life."

"George and Trudy shared the Nobel Prize," Barry said.

"What for?" asked Mary.

"Oh, it's a bit complicated," said Elion. "Basically, we tried to make drugs that would just attack diseased cells in the human body and leave the healthy cells alone. That was the problem with the old cancer treatments. Sometimes they caused more harm than good." Trudy looked sad and Mary wondered if she was thinking of her grandfather.

"The drugs we made are used to treat lots of diseases now. Leukaemia, malaria, herpes, even HIV/AIDS. They also help people who need organ transplants. Your body thinks that an organ that has come from another person, especially if they aren't related to you, is a dangerous intruder. It does everything it can to reject it, which is bad news if you have kidney or liver failure or need a new heart from a donor to survive. Our drugs stop the new organ from being rejected."

Elion fumbled in a handbag for a minute and pulled out a crumpled envelope. "Forget the awards and honours, Mary. This is the best piece of paper I have ever received. It arrived a few weeks ago. It's a letter from a lady who had a kidney transplant sixteen years ago and was given our drug. She saw

George's obituary in the newspaper and wrote to me. She says, 'My life is full of joy because of your discoveries'."

Mary thought Elion might be about to cry, but instead a fierce, determined look appeared on her face and she looked exactly like she did when she was fifteen.

"People ask me if I was aiming for a Nobel Prize all my life. That would be crazy. What if you didn't get it? Your whole life would be wasted. What we were aiming at was getting people well, and the satisfaction of that is much greater than any prize."

She looked sharply at Mary.

"Don't waste your life chasing awards, young lady. Do the work you want to do. Then it won't seem like work at all. And don't be afraid if it's hard. Nothing worthwhile comes easily."

The Nobel Prize in Physiology or Medicine 1988 was awarded jointly to Sir James Black, Gertrude Elion and George Hitchings 'for their discoveries of important principles for drug treatment'.

LATE BLOOMERS

Like Gertrude Elion, Guglielmo Marconi and Youyou Tu, not all Nobel Prize winners have high-level formal qualifications like a PhD. Despite only having a master's degree, Jack Kilby (Physics, 2000) managed to invent the computer microchip, handheld calculator and thermal printer. Koichi Tanaka (Chemistry, 2002) only managed to get a bachelor's degree, and failed several exams while at university. Charles Pederson (Chemistry, 1987) decided to get a job instead of studying for a PhD because he didn't want to be rely on his father to support him.

Others did quite badly at school. John Gurdon's (Physiology or Medicine, 2012) school report for Biology, which he failed, says that his ambition to become a scientist was ridiculous. His teacher wrote it 'would be a sheer waste of time, both on his part, and of those who have to teach him'. Gurdon framed the report and hung it above his desk.

INVISIBLE INK

Important letters, like the one Gertrude Elion received, can sometimes be kept for a very long time. But if you want the message in your letter to be a secret, you could make this invisible ink.

WHAT YOU NEED

- Baking soda
- Water
- Container
- 2 cotton buds
- Purple grape juice concentrate (or strong hibiscus tea)
- Paper

WHAT TO DO

1. Put equal amounts of the baking soda and water (try ¼ cup of each) into the container and stir until all the soda is dissolved.

2. Dip the cotton buds in the mixture and write a message on the paper.

3. Leave it to dry. The message you have written will be invisible.

4. Using a clean cotton bud, paint all over the paper with the grape juice concentrate to reveal the message.

WHAT TO LOOK FOR

We measure how acidic a substance is using the pH scale, which goes from 0 to 14. Water is neutral, so it has a pH of 7. A substance with a pH lower than 7 is called an 'acid'. A substance with a pH higher than 7 is called a 'base'.

pH indicators are substances that change colour when they touch different pHs. Grape juice concentrate is a pH indicator. Baking soda is a base. When grape juice concentrate touches a base, it turns from purple to green.

Your invisible message will appear on the paper as green letters.

10

FEEDING THE WORLD

Norman Borlaug

Mary opened her eyes and immediately shut them again. The world had suddenly become very, very bright. Also quite hot, she realised, which was a nice contrast to the cold cemetery they had landed in last time. She opened her eyes, more cautiously this time. She was standing in the middle of a field, surrounded by green and golden plants that were swaying in a gentle breeze. The plants, which were all exactly the same height, came up to her waist. One tickled her hand and she plucked off its golden tip.

The patch she was standing in was perfectly square. Straight paths were cut through the crop, from top to bottom and left to right, as far as she could see, dividing it into neat, square sections.

Each square had a wooden sign firmly hammered into the ground at its edge. The sign closest to her read 'SONORA-64'.

"Barry, what's a sonora?" she asked, looking around for him. She spotted him striding along a pathway, heading for a group of people who were gathered around a bright red tractor. "Barry! Wait for me," she called, and she set out after him.

By the time she caught up with Barry, he was talking to the man sitting in the driver's seat of the tractor. Like everyone else, except Mary and Barry, he was wearing a white, short-sleeved shirt, shorts, workboots and a wide-brimmed straw hat.

"Drink?" Barry asked, passing her a tin flask. Mary suddenly realised how dry her throat was and she gulped the cool water gratefully. When she finished, she handed the flask back to the man.

"Thank you, Mr ... "

"Borlaug. Norman Borlaug," he said, jumping down from the tractor to stand beside her. "So, Mary, you want to win a Nobel Prize. Why?"

No one had ever asked Mary that before and she thought carefully before answering. "I guess because it would mean that I had discovered something new and important. Something that helps us understand the world."

"Fair enough," said Borlaug. "Understanding is good. But what about saving the world? Saving lives!"

"A billion lives," said Barry. "That's what they're saying, Norman. Your work saved more than a billion people from starving to death. Mary, they call him the father of the Green Revolution."

Borlaug looked embarrassed. "I hate that name. I was only ever one of many people ... "

"So, are these plants your discovery?" asked Mary.

"They're wheat," said Borlaug. "We're developing new varieties that give the farmers a better yield. That means they can use the same amount of land, but grow twice as much as they did before. Now they don't have to cut down forests to get more farmland to grow more food. In some countries, we have doubled the amount of wheat farmers can produce."

"Amazing," said Barry. "When they started growing Norman's wheat in India, there was so much of it that they couldn't cope. They ran out of people to harvest it, bags to store it in, carts to haul it from the farms to the markets and trucks to drive it around the country. In some places, they even had to close schools to use the buildings as warehouses for all the extra wheat."

"Only temporarily," added Borlaug. "That all settled down quite quickly."

"And Mexico, where we are now," Barry continued, "went from being a country where people were starving to one that had so much wheat that it sold what it didn't need to the rest of the world."

"Were people really starving?" asked Mary.

"Oh, yes," said Barry. "We're in 1960 now, and the population of the planet has exploded in the past few decades. The world is in crisis. The predictions are for a massive, worldwide famine. Without Norman's work, there won't be enough food to feed everyone."

"I grew up on a farm," said Borlaug. "I remember the Great Depression. There was a drought and the crops failed. All the soil on the farms blew away in a terrible dust storm. People starved then. I couldn't bear to see that happen again on a bigger scale across the whole world. That's why I decided to work with crops. This is our test farm. Each square plot has a different variety planted in it, or is being grown using a different method or under different conditions. We're trying everything we can to get more grains.

That one you have in your hand is called Sonora-64."

Mary blushed and shoved the offending plant into her pocket.

"Oh, no, that's OK," said Borlaug. "Have a close look at it. Did you notice all the plants are the same size? That's to make sure they all get an equal share of sunlight. And they're quite small, too. Larger plants don't produce more grains of wheat, they just use up energy growing taller. We want short, compact plants that have fat, plump grains on them. The more, the better. Sometimes when the wind is blowing across the field, you can hear the wheat rubbing together. It's like music. Once you hear it, you never forget it."

"How do you get the wheat plants to be short and fat?" asked Mary.

"Cross-breeding, genetics and fertilisers," said Borlaug. "And we're trying to make the plants resistant to disease and pests as well."

"So which Nobel Prize did you win?" asked Mary. "I don't suppose it's Physics. Was it for Chemistry?"

Borlaug looked embarrassed again. "Peace," he mumbled. "They gave me the Peace Prize. It's a bit silly, really. When my wife drove to the fields where I was working to tell me, I didn't believe her at first. A pack of photographers followed her so they could take pictures of me working and they trampled all the wheat. And she said I had to go and buy a suit. It was all very annoying, really."

"I didn't know a scientist could win a Peace Prize," said Mary.

"Well, you can't build a peaceful world on

empty stomachs and human misery," said Borlaug. "In 1950, there were two and a half billion people on the planet. Now, in 1960, there are three billion. Barry, I know you aren't meant to tell me, but what is the population of the world in 2017?"

"Seven and a half billion," said Barry.

Borlaug shook his head sadly. "You might need to think of something else," he said. "Maybe that can be your job, Mary."

✳ ✳ ✳

The 1970 Nobel Peace Prize was awarded to Norman Borlaug.

THE OTHER NOBELS

Nobel Prizes are awarded for Literature and Peace as well as Physics, Chemistry and Physiology or Medicine (today, we would just call this last category 'Biology'). In 1969, the Nobel Memorial Prize in Economic Sciences was added. There has never been a Nobel Prize for mathematics, probably because Alfred Nobel was a very practical scientist and engineer who didn't think that maths was as important as the other sciences.

Only one person has won Nobel Prizes for their work in both science and peace. Linus Pauling won the 1954 Chemistry prize for his research into chemical bonds. He was invited to help develop the first atomic bomb but he was frightened that a nuclear war would destroy humanity. He and his wife persuaded 11,000 scientists to sign a petition calling for an end to nuclear weapon tests. On the very day that the first treaty banning nuclear testing was signed, he was awarded the 1962 Nobel Peace Prize.

WHOLEWHEAT BANANA MUFFINS

Norman Borlaug's discovery helped to feed millions of people by making it easier for them to grow more wheat. Wheat is a very important food. It contains 50 per cent more protein than rice, so it is more nutritious. It is used to make bread, pasta, breakfast cereal and lots of baked goods. This recipe uses kernels of whole wheat, which are called wheat berries or wheat grain, to make a healthy snack.

WHAT YOU NEED

- 1½ cups wheat grain (you can buy this from health food stores)
- 2 teaspoons baking powder
- ¼ teaspoon cinnamon
- ¾ cup sugar
- 1 egg
- 2 mashed bananas
- ¼ cup vegetable oil
- Coffee grinder or mortar and pestle
- Oven
- 2 mixing bowls
- Muffin tray
- Paper muffin cases

WHAT TO DO

1. Preheat the oven to 180°C.

2. Put the muffin cases into the tray.

3. Put the wheat berries into your coffee grinder or mortar and pestle. You might not be able to fit them all in at once.

4. Grind the wheat berries into a fine flour.

5. Mix the flour, baking powder, cinnamon and sugar in the bowl. Make a well in the middle of the bowl.

6. In another bowl, beat the egg and stir in the banana and oil.

7. Pour the banana mixture into the flour. Stir until all the dry ingredients are completely mixed in.

8. Spoon the mixture into the muffin cases, leaving some room at the top.

9. Bake the muffins in the oven for 15–20 minutes. Cool before eating.

WHAT TO LOOK FOR

A grain of wheat has three layers. The hard, outer layer is the bran. This is where most of the fibre and nutrients are. The next layer is the germ. This is oily and contains lots of vitamins, proteins and minerals. The inside is the endosperm, which is mostly made of starch.

These wholewheat muffins are very good for you because they use all of the wheat grain. Flour that you buy in the shop is only made from the endosperm.

11

LADY OF THE CELLS

Rita Levi-Montalcini

"Hurry, we're late," said Barry as he rushed up a stone staircase at the front of a huge old building.

Mary had to run to keep up with him. "You really need to get the hang of that time machine. Maybe I could work it?" she panted.

"Absolutely not," he shouted over his shoulder. "Come on! The party's already started." He ran through an open door and disappeared into the building.

Annoyed, Mary stopped at the top of the stairs and turned to look back the way they had come. Just below her was a plaza paved in grey and white stone. In the centre, on a white stone pedestal, stood a larger-than-life bronze statue of a man in a robe, with a wreath on his head, astride a powerful horse. The man's right arm was outstretched, as if he was addressing an invisible crowd. Buildings stretched out below her, many with domes on top. It was evening and the lights of the city were starting to come on. People were sitting at outdoor tables, drinking wine and smoking cigarettes, or strolling through narrow lanes holding ice-cream cones. A plane flew overhead so she knew that, although the city looked ancient, they had not travelled very far back in time.

The sound of hundreds of voices singing in unison drifted out from the open door. "*Tanti auguri a te! Tanti auguri a te! Tanti auguri a Rita! Tanti auguri a te!*" The words weren't familiar but the tune was. It was someone's birthday. And that meant cake, Mary thought, realising she was actually quite hungry. She turned her back on Rome and entered the building.

Inside, a party was in full swing. At the centre of the room was the oldest person Mary had ever seen. She was wearing a white shirt and a black jacket that fitted her tiny frame perfectly. Her pure white hair sat on her head like a perfectly sculpted wave. There was a gold brooch at her throat and her wrinkled hands were laden with bracelets and rings. In front of her was a cake decorated with chocolate curls and fresh raspberries. In her right hand she held a knife and in her left she had a champagne glass that was full to the top. As Mary watched, the woman simultaneously cut the cake and sipped the champagne, without spilling a drop. She noticed Mary watching and gave her a wink then gestured to her to come closer.

"You are wondering how old I am, young Mary."

"No, I wasn't!" said Mary, although that was exactly what she had been thinking.

"I am one hundred years old today. I was born

in 1909. My colleagues in the Roman Senate have thrown me this party. I am the oldest living Nobel Prize winner and the only one to ever reach this age. Apparently that makes me special. Cake?"

Mary accepted gratefully. Just as she took a mouthful of a massive slice of the cake, Barry noticed her. "Ah, Mary, there you are. What took you so long? Have you met Rita Levi-Montalcini? She's a legend!"

"Mm-hm," mumbled Mary through the cake.

"How old are you, Mary?" asked Rita.

"Ten," said Mary, swallowing the last of her mouthful and looking longingly at the rest of the cake on her plate. "And three-quarters," she added, hoping the extra months made her sound a bit more grown-up.

"You have many years ahead of you then. And the world is a very different place now. When I was ten and three-quarters, my twin sister and I were not meant to become anything more than wives and mothers." She snorted loudly. "I had no interest in that life. I never married. I became a doctor instead. I was working as an assistant in the anatomy department of a university, researching the nervous system, when I was dismissed."

"Because you were a woman?" asked Mary.

"No, my dear. Because I was Jewish. It was 1938. Those were dark days, but darker ones were to come. During World War II, I created a laboratory in my bedroom so I could continue my work in secret. I made surgical instruments out of sharpened sewing needles. When the Germans invaded Italy, I fled with my family to Florence and I worked from a corner of our living room. Oh, Mary, you should have seen it. There were eggs everywhere!"

"Eggs?"

"I was trying to find out how cells grow and develop. To do my research, I needed chicken embryos. For that, you need eggs. During the war, there was a shortage of eggs. I had to ride my bicycle around the countryside and persuade the farmers to sell them to me." Rita took another huge gulp of her champagne. "An embryo starts with a single cell. And from that one cell comes everything that makes up your entire body, in all its wonderful complexity. Your skin, and hair and nails. Your heart, liver, kidneys and lungs. Your eyes and the gift of sight! Not to mention your magnificent brain, Mary! Haven't you ever wondered how that happens?"

"I guess so," said Mary, wondering about that for the very first time in her life.

"Later in my career, when I was working in America with my dear friend Stanley Cohen, we were able to show that cells send out nerve fibres that connect and communicate with other cells that are nearby, allowing them to work together to create and sculpt organs. It took many years, but we were able to work out how cells talk and listen to each other."

"Rita's work was the start of some very important discoveries," said Barry. "Her research has made it possible for new work to be done on things like birth deformities, dementia and even cancer."

"They call me 'Lady of the Cells'. When I returned to Italy, the President made me a Senator," said Rita. "That means I'm a politician."

"No wonder they're throwing you this big party," said Mary.

"Pfft," Rita snorted, sipping her champagne again. "They are all amazed that I am so old. They have come to look at the hundred-year-old woman. But I don't *feel* old. I am not my body, I am my mind, and it is even better now than when I was 20."

Rita put her glass down and looked fiercely at Mary.

"I hear you want to make your own discoveries. You must learn to be fearless. Don't be afraid to make your own decisions about your future. Don't fear difficult times. They will happen to you, like they do to all of us. The best comes from them. I have never had any regrets." She stood and stretched, surveying the party. "Now, I must join my friends. There is no time to waste, although I still have a few years left in me." Rita winked at Mary again, picked up her drink and walked away. Within seconds the crowd had swallowed her up.

"Wow," said Mary. "She's kind of amazing, isn't she?"

"One of a kind," agreed Barry.

The Nobel Prize in Physiology or Medicine 1986 was awarded jointly to Stanley Cohen and Rita Levi-Montalcini 'for their discoveries of growth factors'. Levi-Montalcini was still publishing scientific papers until the year before her death in 2012, at the age of 103.

A ROCKY ROAD

Levi-Montalcini, like many people, had to overcome many obstacles that had nothing to do with tricky science on her way to a Nobel Prize. Carol Greider (Physiology or Medicine, 2009) struggled through her early years at school. Her dyslexia meant that she was a poor speller, and she was put into remedial classes and found it hard to get good marks.

Gerty Cori and her husband, Carl (Physiology or Medicine, 1947), collaborated throughout their working lives. Despite this, she was paid a salary that was just one-tenth of her husband's and several institutions refused to allow them to work together.

Levi-Montalcini was also not the only scientist to be affected by World War II. In 1938 and 1939, Hitler refused to allow three German winners to accept their Nobel Prizes.

THE DISAPPEARING EGGSHELL

Like Rita Levi-Montalcini, you can also do a simple experiment just using eggs.

WHAT YOU NEED

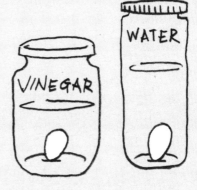

· 2 eggs
· 2 glass jars with lids
· White vinegar
· Permanent marker

WHAT TO DO

1. Carefully put each egg into a container.
2. Fill one jar with vinegar until it completely covers the egg.
3. Fill the other jar with water.
4. Put the lids on the jars.
5. Label each container 'WATER' or 'VINEGAR'.

6. After 24 hours, carefully tip out the liquid and refill it.

7. After another 24 hours, carefully remove the eggs. Wash off any vinegar with water.

WHAT TO LOOK FOR

The egg that has been in the water will not change. But the egg in the vinegar gradually loses its shell.

Vinegar is an acid. It wears away the eggshell by turning the calcium carbonate in the shell into calcium, which floats off into the liquid, and carbon dioxide, which is a gas. You will see this gas as tiny bubbles that form on the outside of the egg.

The shell-less egg is now only held together by a thin membrane. Unlike a shell, this membrane can bend. The egg can even be dropped a few centimetres without breaking. Try this, very carefully, for yourself.

You can repeat this experiment and leave the egg for even longer. Try it with small bones or sea shells and see what happens to them.

12

TINY MACHINES

Sauvage, Stoddart and Feringa

Now they were at the very back of a large concert hall. In the audience, 1500 people sat in chairs covered in red velvet. All the men wore tuxedos with white bow ties and the women were dressed in very formal gowns. The hall sparkled as light danced off sequins, jewellery, medals slung around necks on ribbons, and many, many pairs of spectacles. Every surface was decorated with thousands of pink flowers and flags representing all the countries of the world hung from the balconies.

"I thought you might like to see a Nobel Prize ceremony," said Barry. "This is the formal announcement of the winners. It's a very posh event."

Mary looked down at her clothes, which were now very crumpled and a bit dirty from all of their clumsy landings in dusty rooms and damp grass. She felt very under-dressed for the occasion.

On the centre of the stage, directly behind a large white N that was woven into the dark blue carpet, was a statue of a man's head. "That's Alfred Nobel himself," said Barry. "The ceremony is always held on 10 December, the anniversary of his death."

On either side of the statue sat the judges and previous winners. At the front, on the left, was an empty row of red seats. On the right were six fancy blue and gold chairs for the king of Sweden and his family.

"Sweden has a king?" asked Mary.

"Oh, yes," said Barry. "King Carl XVI Gustaf. Here he comes." An elderly man with thinning grey hair, wearing a black suit covered in fancy medals, walked onto the stage and sat in the largest blue seat.

"He's not wearing a crown," said Mary, a bit disappointed.

The orchestra began to play and eight men walked onto the stage in single file and sat down on the red seats.

"Who's missing?" asked Mary, noticing one red seat was still empty.

"The Literature winner," said Barry. "He's quite shy. He doesn't like ceremonies."

After some speeches, which Mary privately thought went on a bit too long, and some more music from the orchestra, the ceremony got to the point.

A smiling, round-faced man stood at the lectern and looked out at the crowd. He seemed to be having some trouble containing his happiness, as if he was on the verge of doing a little dance or breaking into song.

"Ladies and gentlemen! The 2016 Nobel Prize in Chemistry is all about outstanding imagination, creativity and breaking completely new grounds in science." He beamed. "The prize is awarded to Jean-Pierre Sauvage, Sir Fraser Stoddart and Bernard Feringa for the design and synthesis of molecular machines."

Mary nudged Barry. "What's a molecular machine?"

"Listen," he whispered.

The man continued joyously. "The tiniest machines you can imagine. You could fit a thousand of them across the width of a human hair."

"What's the point of that?" asked Mary.

"Ssshh," said Barry.

One by one, the three new Nobel laureates stood and walked to the large white 'N', shook the King's hand, accepted their gold medal and certificate, bowed to the king, the people behind them and the audience, and then returned to their seat as the orchestra played a triumphant fanfare.

"It's heavier than it looks," Barry whispered when one man nearly dropped his medal on the King's foot.

"Is that all you get?" asked Mary.

"And one million dollars," said Barry.

"One million!" squealed Mary. "Each?" A few people turned and glared at her.

"Ssshh!" said Barry again. "It sounds like a lot, but many winners use it to fund their research. And

if you share the prize, you share the money too. Anyway, those three are the people I want you to meet. Let's go."

They left the room just as a tall slim woman with long grey hair stood up in front of the orchestra. "Oh, where have you been, my blue-eyed son?" she sang.

"We'll have to be quick," said Barry, ushering Mary down a flight of stairs to a large foyer and then into a small room that was crammed full with heavy winter coats and handbags. "The winners are about to go to the dinner."

"Barry! Check this out!" cried a tall man as he rushed into the room waving a medal.

Mary recognised Sauvage from the medal ceremony. He was followed into the cloakroom by Stoddart and Feringa, and she realised they were the three men who were learning the rules of the secret society she had stumbled into.

When was that, she wondered? It felt like it had just happened a few hours ago, but really it was probably sometime in the future. Her head ached a little thinking about it.

"Congratulations!" said Barry, shaking their

hands vigorously. "It's a great feeling, isn't it? I know you've got to rush off to the dinner, but Mary wants to know what your tiny molecular machines can be used for."

"That's the beauty of it, Mary," said Stoddart. "We don't know yet. One hundred years ago, when the Wright brothers built the first flying machine, they couldn't have imagined that one day people would fly around the world in a single day, let alone land on the moon. This is the start of an entirely new era of technology. The opportunities are endless!"

"Imagine tiny robots that can be injected into your veins, and then go in search of cancer cells and deliver the medicine exactly where it's needed," said

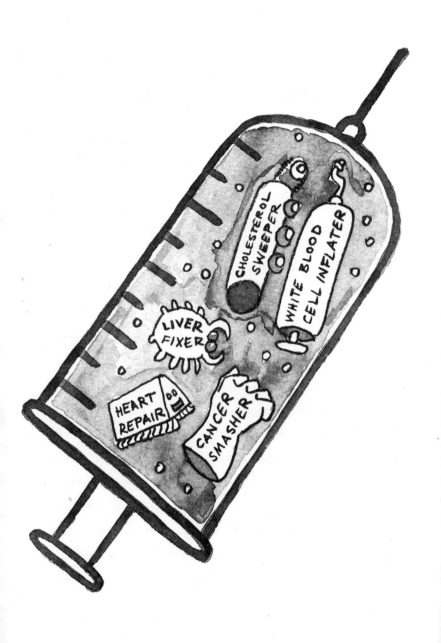

Feringa. "Machines that live inside your body and can monitor how well your heart is working or build you new muscles."

"Or smart materials," added Stoddart. "Bridges that have their own microscopic machines that can run around rebuilding and strengthening them as they get damaged or worn. Plastic pipes that can repair themselves underground. Space stations that build themselves."

"They're like super ants," said Sauvage. "We built a molecular motor that was powered by light and could rotate an object 10,000 times its own size."

"How do you make something that small?" asked Mary.

"It's a bit like building a Lego castle in the dark with boxing gloves," said Feringa. "Except with molecules instead of the bricks, and using chemical reactions as your tools. Sauvage started everything by working out how to link molecules into a chain. Then Stoddart built a molecular wheel and I worked out how to make a motor. And now someone has built a car that is made out of a single molecule."

A loud chime rang out and they heard the

sound of people talking and laughing as they made their way out of the concert hall.

"Dinner!" said Stoddart. "We have to be off, Mary. See you at the next meeting."

"Yes, we better rush. I hear we're having quail with cloudberry sorbet," said Sauvage hurriedly, standing on Stoddart's foot.

"We're late too," said Barry, yanking the time machine from his pocket and frantically spinning the dial.

"But we've got the time machine," said Mary. "How could we *ever* be late? And what meeting will I be at?"

Barry pressed the button and the cloakroom disappeared.

✳ ✳ ✳

The 2016 Nobel Prize in Chemistry was awarded jointly to Jean-Pierre Sauvage, Sir Fraser Stoddart and Bernard Feringa 'for the design and synthesis of molecular machines'.

FUTURE SCIENCE

It's impossible to guess what scientific breakthroughs lie in our future. The next Nobel Prizes could go to the people who find life in space, discover a cure for cancer or work out how to generate enough clean energy to power all of our cities without damaging the environment.

Richard Roberts (Physiology or Medicine, 1993) believes the field that holds the most potential for new discoveries is biology. We still know relatively little about it and, because of evolution, it is always changing.

If, like Mary, you want to win a Nobel Prize, it's best to forget about awards and concentrate on doing the very best science you can. Ask good questions, use innovative methods to answer them, and look for results that reveal an unexpected aspect of nature. And be very, very lucky.

HOW SMALL IS A MOLECULE?

Imagine a grain of sand. Now imagine cutting it in half, then in half again and again and again. When you can't cut the grain of sand any smaller, you have an atom. An atom is the smallest possible piece of something. A group of atoms joined together is called a molecule. Atoms and molecules are too small to see without a special microscope, but this experiment lets you measure the thickness of a single layer of molecules.

WHAT YOU NEED

- Water
- 1 teaspoon fine powder (talcum powder, cornflour or plain flour)
- Olive oil
- Medicine dropper
- Large bowl or dish (at least 20cm diameter)
- Fine sieve
- Ruler
- Calculator

1. Fill the bowl with water.

2. Put a teaspoon of powder into the sieve and, very carefully, dust the water with a very thin layer of powder. Blow gently to remove any spare powder.

3. Put one drop of oil on top of the powder.

4. Watch as the oil spreads out over the surface of the water. This might take a few minutes. If your oil reaches the side of your bowl, you will need to try again with a bigger bowl.

5. Measure the width of the circle of oil. This is called the diameter. Half of the diameter is called the radius.

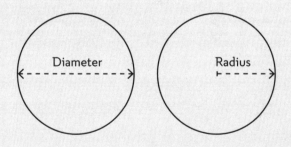

6. Using the formula below, calculate how thick the layer of oil is.

Diameter of circle (mm) = _____

Radius of circle (mm) = diameter ÷2 = _____mm

Volume of drop* = _____ml

* Most medicine droppers give a drop of 0.05ml.

Thickness of oil layer

    = volume of drop x 3.14 x radius x radius

    = _____ml

WHAT TO LOOK FOR

The layer of oil is one molecule thick. One molecule of olive oil is about 0.000002 mm thick. How close was your answer?

13

TRUST YOUR GUT

Barry Marshall and Robin Warren

Barry and Mary were again standing in the long corridor, outside the storage room.

"Well, that's it," said Barry. "And I've got a meeting to get to." He checked his watch.

"Wait! There's one more person," said Mary. "You haven't told me how you won *your* Nobel Prize."

"Oh, it's not that interesting," said Barry, looking a bit embarrassed. "And it was a team effort. Anyway, I have to return the time machine now."

"Hello, Mary," said a man with white hair and a friendly smile who was walking down the corridor towards them. "I'm Robin Warren. I won the Nobel Prize with Barry. Your mother told me you were keen to talk to him about our work. I thought I might find you here. Did you forget to lock the door again, Barry?"

Barry shrugged his shoulders. "It was just a quick meeting to welcome the newcomers. I didn't expect anyone to be poking around."

"But I was. And I saw everything. So we made a deal," said Mary firmly. "And now I want to know how you won your Nobel Prize."

Barry checked his watch. "I really need to rush off—"

"Barry, just tell her what you did," said Robin.

Barry stared at his feet.

Robin sighed. "Oh, all right, I'll tell her. We were working on stomach ulcers. Horrible things. They give you terrible stomach pain and can make you vomit and lose weight. And they're very common. About one in every ten people will get one. They can lead to stomach cancer and, in the worst cases, you can end up with a hole in your stomach. Some people even bleed to death. For years, doctors thought that stomach ulcers were caused by stress, eating spicy foods or having too much acid in your stomach. They treated their patients by giving them medicine to get rid of the stomach acid."

"It was a huge industry," said Barry. "Some companies made billions of dollars a year from those medicines. They didn't actually work, but the companies weren't interested in finding a different kind of treatment. I asked them for some money to do my research, but they said they couldn't afford it." He snorted.

Robin continued. "When Barry and I met, we began to suspect that the cause might actually be a special kind of bacteria."

"Everyone thought we were mad," said Barry. "No one believed that bacteria could survive in the stomach. It was a 'known fact'."

Both men laughed. "Watch out for those 'known facts', Mary. They can really hold you back," said Robin.

"Like thinking that the earth is flat," said Barry. "Or that carrots help you see in the dark."

"Or that Pluto is a planet," added Mary.

"Pluto *is* a planet," said Barry, looking confused.

"Not anymore," said Mary.

"Anyway," said Robin. "They were wrong. This bacteria not only survived in the stomach, it grew. It's a weird shape, a bit like a corkscrew, and it's tough. But do you know what kills bacteria, Mary?"

Mary remembered what Alexander Fleming had discovered. "Antibiotics!" she said.

Barry beamed proudly. "Correct. So, in theory, if you give someone with a stomach ulcer the right kind of antibiotics, you can kill the bacteria and get rid of the ulcers."

"The problem was that no one believed us," continued Robin. "They were still stuck on this idea that ulcers were caused by stress. They gave patients antidepressants or cut out bits of their stomach. Our idea was too weird for them to take seriously. We couldn't experiment on mice, because they don't get stomach ulcers, and we weren't allowed to do any tests on people."

Barry checked his watch again. "Oh, look at the time. I really must run—"

Robin reached out and grabbed onto his sleeve. "So Barry here took matters into his own hands. Without telling anyone – not even his wife – he deliberately drank some of the bacteria."

Mary stared at Barry in disbelief. "That's crazy!"

"Yes," agreed Robin. "And tell Mary where you got it from, Barry."

Barry shuffled his feet and looked down at the ground and mumbled something too quietly for Mary to hear.

"Louder, Barry," said Robin.

"A *patient*!" Barry shouted. "I got it from the gut of one of my sick patients."

Mary felt a bit sick herself.

"And then what happened?" prompted Robin.

"I was okay for a couple of days," said Barry. "And then I started to feel terrible. I got queasy, my breath smelled horrible, I had terrible stomach pains and then I started vomiting." He grimaced. "It really hurt. But you know what I did next? I took antibiotics and I cured myself."

"And now antibiotics are the standard treatment for stomach ulcers, and almost no one in the Western world gets stomach cancer," said Robin. "Lots of people who could be dead are alive and well, and there's much less suffering in the world."

Robin held out his hand to Mary. "It was lovely

meeting you. I'm sure we'll bump into each other again one day." He winked at Barry.

"Goodbye," said Mary, shaking his hand.

"I have to go too," said Barry. "But did you learn everything you wanted to know, Mary? Do you still want to win a Nobel Prize now that you know how much hard work it is and how long it can take for your discoveries to be recognised?"

Mary thought for a while. "I'm not sure. I used to think that if I won a Nobel Prize I'd suddenly be rich and famous. I guess it doesn't always work out that way. But I would like to help people, like you did. You know what I'm really interested in now? That time machine you have. Could I have a quick look at it, just to see how it works?"

Barry took a few steps back. "Oh, no, I couldn't let you do that. There's rules about who can use it. And, to be honest, I'm not entirely sure how it works myself. I couldn't explain it to you. Most of the time I just press the buttons and hope for the best."

"But just imagine what you could do with it!" said Mary. "We could go back in time and cure diseases, or find new sources of energy that don't pollute the planet or stop animals from becoming extinct—"

"Not dinosaurs," said Barry, looking alarmed. "That's why there has to be rules."

"I guess so," said Mary, a bit disappointed. "But I would like to hold it."

Barry's shoulders drooped and he looked down at Mary. "OK, you can hold it this once. But you have to promise you won't press any buttons."

"I promise!" said Mary, and Barry fished the machine out of the pocket of his lab coat and put it into her hands. She held it carefully. It was heavier than she had expected and it felt warm and smooth all over, except for a tiny raised area that she could feel on the back which felt rough. She touched that with her fingers and, when Barry took his eyes off her to glance at his watch, she flipped the machine over to have a closer look. On the back was a very small plaque. Engraved on it were the words, "To Barry from Mary".

Barry looked up, let out a squawk and snatched the time machine from her hands. "OK, now it's really time for me to go, before I get into trouble again for being late. But I'll see you again, Mary.

You can count on that."

Barry rushed off through the main door to the research centre, leaving Mary deep in thought. "If time is curved, and if you could find a way to travel faster than light, and if you could build something like a space ship that was so small that it could fit in your hand, I wonder what would happen if ... " she said slowly to herself.

172

"Mary! There you are!" Mary's mother was waving at her from the door that Barry had just gone through. "I've been looking everywhere for you. Professor Marshall said he thought you might be out here. He's *finally* turned up for our meeting. Do you mind waiting here for a while? I won't be too long."

"That's fine. I've got some stuff to think about," said Mary, opening the notepad on her phone to start work on the best idea she had ever had.

The Nobel Prize in Physiology or Medicine 2005 was awarded jointly to Barry Marshall and Robin Warren 'for their discovery of the bacterium Helicobacter pylori and its role in gastritis and peptic ulcer disease'.

HUMAN GUINEA PIGS

Barry Marshall and Tu Youyou are not the only Nobel Prize winners to experiment on themselves. Werner Forsmann (Physiology or Medicine, 1956) was working on a way to measure the pressure inside the heart using a thin hollow tube called a catheter. He had successfully experimented on a horse, but wasn't allowed to try with a human being because it was too dangerous. He found a nurse who agreed to help him, on the condition that he experiment on her and not himself. He strapped the nurse to the table, and then quickly inserted the catheter into his own arm and pushed it all the way to his heart.

When Ralph Steinman (Physiology or Medicine, 2011) was diagnosed with pancreatic cancer, he had been working on a way to use the body's own immune cells to fight infection and cancer. He began a human trial, using himself as the patient, and survived much longer than his doctors had predicted.

RED CABBAGE INDICATOR

Helicobacter pylori, the bacteria that causes stomach ulcers, survives in the very acidic environment of our stomach. It does this by producing an enzyme, urease, which breaks urea down into carbon dioxide and ammonia. Ammonia is a weak base that neutralises the stomach acid. Scientists developed a test that tells them if a patient's stomach lining contains urease. If it does, they know the patient is infected with *Helicobacter pylori*.

The test uses a pH indicator. Many pH indicators come from plants. In this experiment, you will make a pH indicator from red cabbage water.

WHAT YOU NEED

- 3 cups chopped red cabbage
- Vinegar
- Baking soda
- Lemon juice
- Dishwashing liquid

- Saucepan
- Sieve
- Jar
- Medicine dropper
- Clear plastic cups

WHAT TO DO

1. Put the cabbage in the saucepan and cover with water.

2. Bring the water to a boil and then turn off the heat. Let it cool down for about 30 minutes.

3. Pour the cabbage water through the sieve into the jar. This is your pH indicator.

4. Fill one cup with water, one with vinegar, and one with a teaspoon of baking soda mixed with water.

5. Put a few drops of the indicator ice cubes into each cup. Watch how the colours change in each one. Fill in the table below.

6. Using a clean cup, repeat with lemon juice. Look at the colour and work out if lemon juice is an acid or a base.

7. Using a clean cup, repeat with dishwashing liquid. Look at the colour and work out if dishwashing liquid is an acid or a base.

8. Now test other liquids that you find around the house, for example, yoghurt, apple juice, mouthwash, toothpaste, milk, soft drinks, cleaning fluids and washing powder. Use a clean cup every time. Guess what colour the solution will be before you drop the ice cube in. Look at the colour and work out whether the liquid is an acid or a base.

Substance	Indicator colour	Acid or base?
Water	_____	Neutral
Vinegar	_____	Acid
Baking soda	_____	Base
Lemon juice	_____	_____
Dishwashing liquid	_____	_____
_____	_____	_____
_____	_____	_____
_____	_____	_____
_____	_____	_____

WHAT TO LOOK FOR

The pH scale goes from 0 to 14. Water is neutral and has a pH of 7. A pH less than 7 is acidic. Vinegar has a pH of 2.4. A pH more than 7 is basic. Baking soda has a pH of 9.

To feel what time travel is like, try taking a 30-minute afternoon "power nap". If you fall deeply asleep, you cannot feel time passing. So when you wake up after 30 minutes, the rest of the universe has moved forward half an hour, but to you it feels like it was just an instant. It's as if you've travelled 30 minutes into the future!

The good thing is that you now feel very refreshed and are able to tackle difficult mental tasks just as easily as you could first thing in the morning. Lots of Nobel Prize winners take power naps and time travel like this – especially me!

Nobody understands why this works, but it's an important question. Actually, the 2017 Nobel Prize in Chemistry was awarded for research into biological clocks – the chemicals that make us sleep at night and wake in the daylight.

AUTHOR NOTE

A young girl named Mary McCusker (aged nine) approached me during a business meeting and asked for my advice on how to win a Nobel Prize. This conversation was the catalyst for writing the book *How to Win a Nobel Prize*. Mary explained to me that she loved doing science experiments in her kitchen, especially those involving slime, fizzy bi-carbonate soda and food dye. Her kitchen experiments reminded me of my own mischievous adventures when I was her age, often in the garden shed.

While Mary and I travel through time in this book, we don't get up to too much trouble. Mary insisted on including experiments that young scientists can do themselves at the end of each chapter. I hope that, like Mary, you enjoy them too!

BARRY MARSHALL won the 2005 Nobel Prize for Medicine, with Robin Warren, for discovering that stomach ulcers can be caused by bacteria and can be treated with antibiotics. He experimented on himself to prove their theory.

LORNA HENDRY is a writer, editor, graphic designer and teacher but, long before all of that, she studied science at university. She loves the challenge of making science fun and easy to understand. Lorna has written books on a range of topics, from endangered animals to genetics. She has never won a Nobel Prize.

BERNARD CALEO discovered the Tintin series of comic books at his local library when he was five, and this shaped his entire life. These days he draws pictures, writes words, and makes comic books.

MARY is in love with science and often raids her mum's pantry for food dye, cornstarch and other experimental bits and pieces to perform her experiments. She is terrible at cleaning up her mess afterwards but would love to follow in the steps of her hero, Professor Marshall, and one day win a Nobel Prize.

THE UNIVERSITY OF
WESTERN
AUSTRALIA | The Marshall Centre

SOME OF THE AUTHOR PROCEEDS FROM THE SALE OF THIS BOOK ARE GOING TO SUPPORT RESEARCH AT THE MARSHALL CENTRE.

The Marshall Centre was set up in 2007 after Professor Barry Marshall and Dr Robin Warren won their Nobel Prize. The Marshall Centre does all sorts of medical research into things like tropical diseases, superbugs and gut problems.

www.marshallcentre.uwa.edu.au

The McCusker Charitable Foundation

The McCusker Charitable Foundation is proud to support the Marshall Centre and the ongoing research of Western Australian Nobel laureates Professor Barry Marshall and Emeritus Professor Robin Warren. We hope that many young girls and boys will follow in their inspiring footsteps after reading this book.